THE COMMUNIST
MANIFESTO

MANIFESTO

WORDS THAT CHANGED THE WORLD
THE COMMUNIST MANIFESTO

David Boyle

First edition for the United States, its territories and possessions, and Canada
published in 2004 by Barron's Educational Series, Inc. by arrangement with the Ivy Press Limited

All inquiries should be addressed to:
Barron's Educational Series, Inc.,
250 Wireless Boulevard
Hauppauge, New York 11788
www.barronseduc.com

International Standard Book Number
0-7641-2838-8

Library of Congress Catalog Card No. 2003111824

This book was conceived,
designed, and produced by
THE IVY PRESS LIMITED
The Old Candlemakers
West Street, Lewes
East Sussex, BN7 2NZ, U.K.

Creative Director Peter Bridgewater
Publisher Sophie Collins
Editorial Director Jason Hook
Designer Alan Osbahr
Picture Researcher Vanessa Fletcher
Project Editor Mandy Greenfield

Printed in China
9 8 7 6 5 4 3 2 1

THE COMMUNIST MANIFESTO

THE COMMUNIST MANIFESTO
INTRODUCTION

Friedrich Engels, a wealthy businessman and communist sympathizer, and probably the only friend Marx managed to keep lifelong. His good sense, tact, and communication skills were a crucial ingredient in the creation of the *Manifesto*.

Eighteen forty-eight was one of those tumultuous years that echo through the pages of history. It was a year of revolution in most of the great capital cities of Europe, with dynasties overthrown, communes declared, and human equality trumpeted from the barricades. So apocalyptic were its effects that they were still being felt more than half a century later at the outbreak of World War I. And of all the revolutionary events of 1848, the publication of the *Communist Manifesto* probably had the most widespread impact on history—though, ironically, very little effect in the year it was actually published.

Communism had existed before 1848, as an uneasy mixture of utopian ideals, socialism, and egalitarianism—described in the *Manifesto* as a "specter" haunting Europe—but until the *Manifesto*'s publication it possessed no agreed shape, philosophy, or program, and was not a single movement. The *Manifesto's* publication in London in February of that year changed all that.

Its authors were two German revolutionaries who spent most of their lives—and died—in England. The political philosopher Karl Marx and the industrialist Friedrich Engels had been collaborating for four years, and had been commissioned by the Communist League in the closing months of 1847. Engels—the better communicator—made the first draft, and deliberately couched it in language that would be understood by the burgeoning industrial workforce that had come to be living in appalling conditions in the new industrial cities of Europe. Marx, who had trouble with deadlines throughout his life, managed to write the final draft by keeping himself going with copious brandy and cigars. The whole process took just six weeks, and it is clear by the foreshortened final chapter that—as always—Marx never quite got around to writing all that he had intended.

The *Communist Manifesto* has been the most readable, most clearly understandable, most challenging, and most inflammatory expression of socialist philosophy ever written. It has been translated into nearly every language in the world and rivals the Bible and the Koran in the extent of its publishing history. The original publication may have been all but overlooked in a world that was already in open revolt, but in the long run, the *Communist Manifesto* influenced and inspired successful revolutionaries, including Lenin, Stalin, Mao, Ho Chi Minh, Castro, Pol Pot, and many others. For much of the middle third of the twentieth century, 40 percent of the world's population was governed by people who professed allegiance to its tenets. By the end of the century many tens of millions had lost their lives in purges ordered directly by leaders who claimed the label "Marxist."

The *Manifesto* is either the most misunderstood, misinterpreted political tract in history, or the most mistaken, depending on your political convictions. But it is also more than just a manifesto: it is an outline for a revolution in history, philosophy, sociology, and politics. As such, it remains important to this day.

Karl Marx, bullish, impecunious, impossible as a friend or colleague, and yet brilliant in his insights into the contemporary world. His stamp on the *Manifesto* meant that the subsequent movement that emerged out of it was ever afterward linked with his name.

THE COMMUNIST MANIFESTO
CONTEXT AND CREATORS

When the authors of the *Communist Manifesto*, Karl Marx and Friedrich Engels, were born, the effects of the first great revolution in Europe were still being felt. The French Revolution of 1789 was the first major social revolution to challenge the old European order. Marx and Engels's parents were part of the first generation to grow up in the knowledge that such radical, sudden, and overwhelming change was possible.

Before 1789, the great nations of Europe—including Prussia, the homeland of both men—had been governed by a powerful monarchy that was supported by the privileged nobility and the clergy. But a new middle class—described as the "bourgeoisie" in the *Manifesto*—was emerging across the continent, and especially in recently industrialized England, while the working class squeezed into the new industrial cities.

Looking back at the French Revolution as they formulated the *Manifesto*, Marx and Engels developed the view that in France at this time the old order was increasingly coming under pressure from the bourgeoisie and from the growing power of money, which was eventually to sweep away aristocratic and ecclesiastical privilege. In France before 1789, it was this bourgeoisie that became more and more disturbed, watching in dismay as the country plunged further into debt to pay for Louis XVI's sumptuous court at Versailles, the whims of his pleasure-loving wife, and his costly foreign wars. This new class provided Louis and France with wealth, and now they

Billowing smoke from the chimneys of the industrial region of England known as the Black Country. The emergence of an industrial proletariat, the new urban poor, in the generation before Marx's birth was the key factor in his new philosophy.

sought a level of influence in government that would ensure that their interests were better served.

The bourgeoisie was joined in its uprising with a class of workers known as the *sans-culottes* (literally, "without knee breeches," because they wore trousers rather than the more modish breeches of the wealthier classes). These craftsmen, skilled and semiskilled workers, took to the streets of Paris to demand bread and other basic economic necessities. When these two groups combined to storm the Bastille on July 14, 1789, it was the first use of violence by peasants and bourgeoisie together to achieve revolutionary aims. They hung from lampposts any aristocrat, government official, or army officer who stood in their way, then they set about destroying 40,000 châteaux and monasteries across France.

According to the *Manifesto*, the French Revolution "abolished feudal property in favor of bourgeois property." This was not, as Marx and Engels made clear, the ultimate revolution—that of the proletariat. But it was a crucial step.

Because Marx and Engels grew up in post-revolutionary Europe, the conviction that political change could come about only through revolution formed the very core of their beliefs. They were convinced that the ruling classes would never willingly give up their power, and this made revolution inevitable. This belief can be seen in contrast to less doctrinaire forms of socialism that believed not in revolution but rather in peaceful evolution toward similar goals.

Top: street protests in Paris during the French Revolution.

Above: a contemporary print of the epoch-making storming of the Bastille in 1789. It was this event that made Marx and Engels believe that revolutionary change was possible.

The execution of the French king, Louis XVI, in 1793: the revolution had spun out of control and descended into bloody chaos and intolerance. The death of the king set the seal on the destruction of French feudalism and aristocracy.

Revolutions have a habit of violence, which threatens to spin out of control. And as the French Revolution achieved more popular support, it also became more intolerant, culminating in the Reign of Terror of 1793–94. During this bloody period, revolutionary tribunals were quick to condemn opponents of the regime to the guillotine, as the revolution "devoured its own." Some 30,000–50,000 people were arrested as "enemies of the state," and many of them died. It was a foretaste of the state violence of totalitarian Marxist regimes in Stalinist Russia and Maoist China.

Feudalism was wiped out in France in one night— August 4, 1789—and members of the National Assembly wept as they gave up their exemptions from taxation, feudal dues, and tithes. Their *Declaration of the Rights of Man and Citizen* sought to abolish the class system, as it declared

A contemporary print of revolutionary women making their way with cannons toward the royal palace of Versailles.

that men could achieve high status whatever their background. The *Declaration* included the principles of freedom of speech, freedom of the press, and freedom from unlawful arrest or imprisonment— all rights that were denied to both Marx and Engels, who were forced to live in exile for most of their lives because of the opinions they expressed in their writings. For revolutionaries in the generations to come, these were critical ideals. But the *Manifesto* had a different approach from the *Declaration*—a self-declared "scientific" one that was supposed to transcend mere morality and prove that the revolution of the proletariat was a historical inevitability.

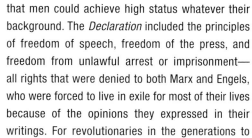

"When France sneezes, Europe catches cold," complained the Austrian foreign minister, Metternich—one of the "bogeymen," along with the French prime minister Guizot, who signed the warrant for Marx's deportation in 1845, and who was singled out for special mention at the start of the *Manifesto*. It was true, as Marx later believed, that revolution was contagious. In 1819 there was a brief liberal revolution in Spain, and there was another in Italy in 1820. The Greek revolution for independence from Turkey in 1821 became a widely celebrated cause, even inspiring the participation of English Romantic poet Lord Byron (who was to lose his life in the fighting). Russia suffered a short and confused revolt in 1825 when liberal and aristocratic factions attempted to influence the succession to the throne. France underwent another revolution in July 1830, a year in which revolution also broke out in Holland.

Old Europe quaked in its boots at the cries of "liberty, equality, fraternity." Much of the international response to these events went into forming coalitions, such as the Congress of Vienna. Diplomats extended discussions in Vienna through the winter of 1814–15, hammering out a new shape for Europe that would hold firm against new revolutionaries. Another conference in 1820, this time in the Austrian city of Troppau, upheld the right of international intervention into the domestic affairs of a nation in order to enforce this resolution. Throughout the years of Marx and Engels's youth, conservative forces across Europe tried to stem the burgeoning tide of nationalism and constitutional

Top: a French republican club, one of the sources of agitation that led to the revolution of 1848.

Above: an evocation of the *Declaration of the Rights of Man and Citizen*, which sought to abolish the class system in France.

reform. Men such as Metternich built complex webs of police informers to defend against revolutionaries such as Marx.

The scene was set for the deluge of 1848, and by then—nearly three generations after the fall of the Bastille—the proletariat whom the *Manifesto* hailed had become all too obvious in grimy slums across Europe.

The Rise of the Working Class

When news of the defeat of Napoleon at Waterloo reached London in 1815, it had traveled no faster overland than had news of Caesar's defeat of the Gauls in the first century B.C. But by the mid-nineteenth century, trains powered by steam moved one mile a minute. The elderly Duke of Wellington was disquieted that the railroads would encourage the working classes—and the revolutionaries whom he feared—to move about. How right he was: in 1848 one group of Belgian revolutionaries attempted to return from Paris to Brussels by train, but were switched to a side-track by railroad engineers and greeted by the army.

The hiss of steam and the clank of iron machinery also sounded the advent of another kind of revolution. The Industrial Revolution had sparked the movement of millions of Europeans from the countryside to the city to work in the manufacture of steel and cotton textiles. People poured in to manufacturing cities such as Manchester and Birmingham in England, Düsseldorf in Germany, and Lyons in France. These were the new urban poor—Marx identified them as the "proletariat" for the first time in the *Manifesto*.

The Battle of Waterloo in 1815. It was almost the last critical event before the coming of the railways across Europe, which permitted the spread of revolutionaries and their ideas with greater ease than ever before.

Manchester's population of 70,000 at the start of the century had doubled by 1831. London set new records for population growth: from 988,000 in 1801 to a staggering 2,363,000 by 1851. Any concept of urban planning was often overwhelmed by the sheer number of arrivals, and there were few basic facilities such as clean water or sewers—and over it all hung the polluted air belching out from the smoking factories.

Nowhere was the impact of the Industrial Revolution on the lives of the new underclass so great as it was in England. Engels, accompanied by his lover, a red-haired Irish factory girl called Mary Burns, was one of the few men of his class to venture into the slums. He described in graphic terms what he saw in Manchester in 1844 in *The Condition of the Working Class in England*: "Masses of refuse, offal and sickening filth lie among standing pools in all directions; the atmosphere ... laden and darkened by the smoke of a dozen tall factory chimneys. A horde of ragged women and children swarm about here, as filthy as the swine that thrive upon the garbage heaps and in the puddles." The book was enormously influential on a political class that was increasingly aware of the urban poor.

Cholera outbreaks were common, as was the new urban-industrial disease of tuberculosis. In some districts, one child in every three died before his or her first birthday. Marx himself experienced this firsthand, losing three of his own children to the diseases of poverty. "If only there were some means by which you and your family could move into a

Top: **England's Liverpool-to-Manchester Railway in 1831, shortly after its opening. The Duke of Wellington expressed the fear that railways would encourage the working classes to move about.**

Above: **a Yorkshire collier, the new proletariat.**

The choking air around the Colebrookdale ironworks in northern England, where pig iron was first produced in 1709. Factories in the middle of the nineteenth century were brutal, exhausting, and terribly unhealthy places.

more salubrious district and more spacious lodgings!" wrote Engels in a letter of condolence on the death of Marx's daughter Franziska.

If this was where the proletariat lived, where they worked was no better. Mass production was set in a new social environment: the factory. Thousands of workers streamed in at dawn and—after a 14-hour day—out again at dusk, six days a week. A government report of 1842 showed that the average age of death for mechanics, laborers, and their families in Manchester was just 17. Industrial accidents were a major cause of dismemberment and other injuries. Young children were employed, their small bodies able to pass more easily through mines and their nimble fingers to keep pace with weaving machinery.

As the *Manifesto* was to observe: "The work of the proletarian has lost all individual character ... He becomes an appendage of the machine." The alienation of humanity in the industrial system was one of the most important concepts developed in the *Manifesto*, and it has survived, in slightly altered form, into the twenty-first century as a modern preoccupation.

The French Revolution had promised liberty for the workers, but the Industrial Revolution provided only enslavement. Yet in both revolutions, according to Marx and Engels, it was the bourgeoisie who came out on top. In particular in industrial England a new breed of "entrepreneur" emerged. The entrepreneurs used their "capital" to bring together the resources, equipment, and

Below: **around the factories a new generation of overcrowded urban slums had grown up.**

Bottom: **slums like the ramshackle houses huddled together in Newcastle, England, in the 1880s were to be the breeding grounds for Marx's revolution.**

laborers needed to make more money. Wealth now meant power as never before. Philanthropy would occasionally trickle down to the working classes, but the attitude of the age was summed up by Cecil Rhodes, who mined diamonds and gold in South Africa and had two African colonies named after him: "Philanthropy is good, but philanthropy at five per cent is better."

The "steam-mill society" had replaced the feudal lord with the "industrial capitalist," and at the heart of it all was a defining contradiction—or so the *Manifesto* claimed: the means of wealth creation was actually the working classes themselves, the downtrodden proletariat.

The *Communist Manifesto* acknowledged the achievements of the bourgeosie, "its wonders far surpassing Egyptian pyramids, Roman aqueducts, and Gothic cathedrals." Marx and Engels embraced the importance of the original revolution by the bourgeoisie, and predicted an initial revolution in Germany, where there was only a small proletariat.

But the early communists believed they were observing the death throes of capitalism. The *Manifesto* predicted that, by driving hitherto isolated workers into mills and factories, modern industry was creating the very conditions in which the proletariat could associate and combine into a dominant force. The bourgeoisie was producing "its own grave-diggers," Marx noted with satisfaction at the end of the first section. "Its fall and the victory of the proletariat are equally inevitable."

The plaque on the wall of Marx's home at 28 Dean Street, in London's Soho district, where the family lived during their first five years in England, watched by a permanent entourage of Prussian spies.

Police States, the Exile Culture, and the Early Communists

In the early part of the nineteenth century, the royal families of Europe were a close-knit clique, often related to each other. Revolution was in the air and they were holding firmly on to their thrones with the help of authoritarian governments, heavy censorship, and a network of spies. Marx's journalism often received particular attention. In 1842, he became editor of the *Rheinische Zeitung*, a liberal newspaper based in Cologne, but the tone of his articles soon attracted the attention of the authorities. An anti-Russian article was read at the court of Tsar Nicholas I. A quiet word in the ear of the Prussian king and the newspaper was shut down.

This was to become a familiar pattern for Marx and many other radicals of the day. In 1848, King Leopold I of Belgium personally signed the royal decree giving Marx 24 hours to leave the country—and never return—soon after he had finished writing the *Communist Manifesto*. In the early 1850s, Prussian police spies practically set up a permanent encampment outside 28 Dean Street in Soho, the Marx family's address during their first five years in London.

Both Marx and Engels, along with other political exiles, moved between the radical hotbeds of Paris, Brussels, Cologne, and London during the 1830s and 1840s. Inspired by both the July Revolution of 1830 in France and the abortive Polish rebellion of 1831, groups of conspirators met to plan armed revolt. Would-be revolutionaries were

Politicians meet in a back room in Trier. Marx's contemporaries, especially those of a revolutionary disposition, found that they were under constant watch and risked arrest or exile without appeal or trial.

imprisoned for distributing banned literature, with comrades often mounting daring attempts to spring them from prison. Both Marx and Engels managed to avoid more than the occasional night in prison, often fleeing a country when news of imminent arrest came. Marx sometimes took the precaution of adopting a pseudonym to avoid detection—"Monsieur Ramboz" was one that he particularly favored.

In Germany in particular there was a vibrant workers' movement, mostly organized in secret societies with the trappings of the old craft guilds. The attempts by European governments to solve the problem of political unrest by deporting the ringleaders to other European countries had the opposite effect to that which they had intended. Radical ideas spread like wildfire, and groups of exiled revolutionaries were the inevitable outcome of an age of repression and reaction. But none of these groups had a coherent plan or unified agenda. Factionalism was rife, and any localized plot or demonstration that they organized could easily be suppressed by the authorities because they were not acting together. In the same way, where communism was espoused, it did not exist as a coherent framework, but as a mish-mash of utopianism, French egalitarianism, and Christian idealism.

The League of Outlaws was one such group. It was one of the earliest communist organizations of this type, and consisted mostly of exiled Germans. It had been founded in Paris in 1834, and its members were largely what Engels referred to as the most "sleepy-headed elements" of the intellectual middle classes. They were left behind when the clandestine League of the Just, with its code words and passwords, split away in 1836. It was later to become the Communist League, the organization that commissioned the *Manifesto*, but at the time it was just one of many similar underground societies.

After the botched Paris uprising of May 1839, some of the League of the Just's leaders fled to London, a city with a reputation for being rather less hostile to foreign political agitators. Here, they set up the respectable-sounding German Workers' Education Association—in reality a front for a secret society headed by three figures: a burly typesetter called Karl Schapper, a witty and diminutive cobbler called Heinrich Bauer, and a watchmaker called Joseph Moll.

Marx met the triumvirate while he was visiting London in 1843. These were the first working-class revolutionaries he had ever encountered, and he was impressed. Their ideology may have been a little vague, but they had built a thriving network of supporters in Switzerland, Germany, and France. Where the workers' associations were declared illegal, their "lodges" masqueraded as choral societies or gymnastic clubs.

In 1846, Marx and Engels set up the Communist Correspondence Committee, operating out of Brussels. Their aim was to link together socialist leaders living in different parts of Europe, keeping in touch with similar groups in London and Paris, as well as in Germany and Switzerland.

Police and protesters confront each other at an attempted rally by the Reform League in London's Hyde Park in 1866. England had the most developed industrial proletariat, but continually frustrated the Marxists by the non-appearance of the predicted revolution.

Marx soon emerged as a "democratic dictator," but numbers of the original committee of 18 began to fall: the group operated like a twentieth-century communist cell, purging anyone suspected of deviation from official correctness.

One of the first to go was Wilhelm Weitling, a German tailor and one of the best-known members of the League of the Just. He was dismissed as a "tearful emotional communist," despised for his "fatuous and vapid sentimentality." Weitling was ousted from the committee at a meeting where Marx leaped from his seat and thumped the table, shouting at him: "Ignorance never yet helped anybody!" The meeting was adjourned in uproar and Weitling emigrated to America soon afterward.

With Weitling out of the way, Engels was dispatched to sort out the League in Paris. He did this by forcing a debate on the pros and cons of communism, to decide whether the Parisian artisans were true communists or just "in favor of the good of mankind." Engels reported to Brussels that the majority were behind him, though it had taken "a little patience and some terrorism" in order to swing the vote.

The last obstacle was London. Marx had refused to join forces with Schapper, Bauer, and Moll until they re-formed themselves as a Communist League. They finally succumbed and agreed to replace their slogan "All Men Are Brothers"—which Marx despised, because it was patently not the way most people felt—with the new "Working Men of All Countries, Unite!" The inaugural meeting of the new

Marx and Engels coupled together in a German poster of 1948, celebrating the centenary of the *Manifesto*. They look alike in this representation, whereas actually their personalities could not have been more different.

Communist League took place in London in June 1846. It was attended by Wilhelm Wolff from Brussels and Engels, who had traveled from Paris. Marx was absent. Invariably penniless, he simply could not afford the fare.

An Unlikely Couple: Marx and Engels

One of the most famous collaborations in history was also one of the most unlikely. On the surface, Marx and Engels were complete opposites, both in character and lifestyle—even in their physical appearance. Karl Marx (1818–83) was squat and swarthy—his nickname was "Moor"—a bourgeois Jewish intellectual often tormented by self-loathing. Friedrich Engels (1820–95) was a typical specimen of Aryan manhood, tall and fair, born into a wealthy family involved in the textile industry. Both men sported big bushy beards for most of their lives.

The pair first met properly in Paris in August 1844. Engels was passing through on his way to Germany, having visited his family's cotton mills in Lancashire. They had met once before when Engels had visited the Cologne offices of the *Rheinische Zeitung* in 1842, but he had been warned about the young editor who "raves as if ten thousand devils had him by the hair." In Paris, after a few drinks in the Café de la Régence and many days of conversation later, Engels summed up the relationship: "Our complete agreement in all theoretical fields became evident and our joint work dates from this time." He was almost the only person with whom Marx ever managed a continuously friendly relationship.

The reading room of the British Library in Bloomsbury, as it was in Marx's lifetime: this was his home from home in London. He admitted that it was subsidies from Engels that allowed him to spend his time there, rather than earning his living from a "trade."

Marx and Engels complemented each other perfectly. Marx had studied law at the University of Bonn and later philosophy at the more heavyweight University of Berlin. He applied his intellectual vigor to studying economics, but lacked a firsthand knowledge of the machinery of capitalism. This is where Engels came in. Engels could not match Marx's erudition, having missed out on a university education, but he knew a thing or two about what he called "vile commerce," thanks to his involvement in the family business. It was Engels who showed Marx the importance of the birthplace of the proletariat—England—when they first visited the country in 1845, at a time when Marx was still focused on Germany.

Engels began sending Marx money almost as soon as they met. Forty years later, Engels wrote that he could not understand "how anyone can be jealous of genius ... We who have not got it know it to be unattainable right from the start; but to be envious of anything like that one must have to be frightfully small-minded." He saw it as his historic duty to support and subsidize his friend so that Marx could concentrate on his writing. For more than 20 years Engels sent regular amounts of small-denomination banknotes, usually pilfered from the petty cash box at the family firm of Engels and Ermen. As a precaution against mail theft, he snipped the notes in two, posting each half in separate envelopes. Marx admitted that without his benefactor he would have been obliged to start a "trade," rather than spend his days in the reading room of the British Library.

Engels in old age: he was a childless bachelor who set up a mistress and her sister in a separate house, and took part in hunting and wine-tasting, while writing books about revolution in his spare time.

The pair led very different lives. Engels had reluctantly gone into business, but saw the advantages of financial security and time off to pursue his other interests—none of which were political. While living in England, he enjoyed many of the trappings of a high bourgeois lifestyle, such as fine wines and riding with the Cheshire hunt. Engels also lived the unfettered life of a childless bachelor, setting up a *ménage à trois* with Mary Burns and her sister in one house, while entertaining the Manchester middle classes in another.

In sharp contrast, Marx was a married man with three surviving children, who spent most of his life in squalid poverty, fending off creditors and attempting to keep his family alive. His energies, and those of his long-suffering wife, were often channeled into taking or retrieving possessions from the pawnshop, or sending begging letters to relatives. The Marx family was spectacularly bad with money, preferring to use whatever windfalls came their way for music lessons or pets for the girls, rather than pay the doctor's bill. The state of penury and chaos in which the household operated took its toll on the health of the whole family, with Marx suffering most of his life from carbuncles and other pains. His only consolation, he told Engels, was that boils were "a disease of the proletariat."

Unlike Marx, Engels was an efficient time manager. He was able both to hold down a full-time job and pen an impressive output of books, letters, and articles in his elegant hand. Marx's handwriting was so impenetrable that only his wife, Jenny, and Engels could decipher it. At least half of the 500 articles that appeared in the *New York Tribune* with the "Karl Marx" byline were in fact written by Engels. While assuming the outward appearance of an English gentleman, Engels acted as a kind of secret agent behind enemy lines, sending Marx confidential details of the cotton trade and expert observations on the state of the international markets.

It was an effective working partnership and a successful friendship. But the strength of their bond is surprising, given Marx's track record with other friends, most of whom soon became sworn enemies, and more often than not the subject of costly libel suits. The pair wrote frequent letters to each other. These would range from matters of philosophy and politics to carping about other comrades, and more intimate matters—Marx spared few gory details on the state of his boils, and Engels boasted about his sexual encounters. They had no secrets from each other.

Their only recorded falling-out involved a letter sent to Engels on the news of the sudden death of Mary Burns. In place of a heartfelt message of condolence, Marx wrote about his own financial woes, ending the letter: "Instead of Mary, ought it not to have been my mother, who is in any case a prey to physical ailments and has had her fair share of life?" Engels sent a cool reply, and Marx was shamed into penning the closest he ever came to an apology for his insensitivity.

When Marx died in 1883, it was Engels who discovered him dead in his armchair. He delivered an emotional eulogy at Marx's burial in Highgate Cemetery, in

Karl Marx in one of the more lucrative periods of his life, and behind him his daughter Jenny. He and his wife (also called Jenny) used windfall cash to buy clothes and other luxuries rather than paying urgent bills.

The great divide between capitalist and proletariat, as seen in the 1870s: the capitalists stand relaxed on the left while the proletariat heave hammers, almost indistinguishable from the giant cogs of the machine.

north London, three days later. "Just as Darwin discovered the law of development or organic nature," he said, "so Marx discovered the law of development of human history." Perhaps. But he could not have done it without his best friend.

Why the *Manifesto* Was Written

More people have read *The Manifesto of the Communist Party*—to give it its full title—than any other political pamphlet in history, but it must have the most misleading title of them all. There was no such party in 1848. The members of the Communist League who commissioned Marx and Engels wanted a "profession of faith"—and the *Manifesto* was what they got.

An early draft or "Creed" written by Engels in June 1847 was composed in a question-and-answer style, borrowed from the Roman Catholic catechism. ("What is communism? Answer: Communism is the doctrine of the conditions for the emancipation of the proletariat. What is the proletariat? Answer: The proletariat is that class of society which procures its means of livelihood entirely and solely from the sale of its labor ..."). The "secret society" format may have suited the now disbanded League of the Just, but Marx and Engels wanted the new Communist League to be frank about its views and intentions. It needed a manifesto that would reflect this revolutionary openness.

In October 1847, Engels found that the socialist Moses Hess had prepared a rival draft entitled "Confession

of Faith." At a meeting of the League in Paris, Engels demolished this document, which smacked of "utopianism" and, worse, scarcely mentioned the proletariat.

The second congress of the Communist League, in November 1847, was held above the Red Lion pub on Great Windmill Street in London's Soho district—historically the gathering point of European refugees. Intense debate raged for ten days, at the end of which Marx and Engels emerged victorious.

The June congress, which Marx had not attended, had stated the League's aims to be the "emancipation of humanity" through the "community of property and its speediest possible practical introduction." Marx and Engels had upgraded this wishy-washy sentiment to a new set of demands. The Communist League was now calling for nothing less than "the overthrow of the bourgeoisie, the rule of the proletariat, the abolition of the old bourgeois society which rests on the antagonism of classes, and the foundation of a new society without classes and without private property." It was a serious acceleration of ambition.

The objectives of the new League had been so drastically altered by Marx and Engels that a new document summarizing these aims was required with the utmost urgency. Engels, with his consummate skills as a committee man, made sure that this task fell primarily to Marx. He realized that, once in Marx's hands, the document would become a good deal more than an appeal from a small organization with fewer than 1,000 members.

Industrial London, which gave birth to the *Manifesto*, with its cramped living quarters and its chimneys and railway engines belching smoke, as seen by the French artist Gustave Doré in the 1870s.

One of the purposes of the document was to define a doctrine—communism. This new definition, though rooted in the wide-ranging discussions that had taken place ever since the French Revolution, was intended to supersede all competing definitions. The *Manifesto* was an attempt to unify a chaos of ideas into a coherent philosophy. Though presented as the creed of a political party, however, it insisted that the communists did not form "a separate party opposed to other working-class parties": its interests were purely those of the workers.

Marx wrote that, so far, "the philosophers have only interpreted the world in various ways; the point is to change it." This was his own reason for writing the *Communist Manifesto*. He poured scorn on "utopian" social reformers who imagined that the best way to change the situation was to establish idyllic working communities far from the smoking factory chimneys. To change the plight of the worker, Marx believed, you had to take part in the historical process of class struggle and fight the capitalists on their own urban turf.

To convince the workers that they must unite, it was necessary to give them a wholly fresh interpretation of history. The *Manifesto* placed the hardships suffered by workers in England, France, and Germany during the Industrial Revolution in a new context. In Marx's view, history was not the story of great individuals or wars between countries. It was the story of the struggle between social classes. In the mid-nineteenth century this meant the factory owners and the proletariat, who were forced to sell their labor to them. Once the workers gained this consciousness, they would join together to forcefully overthrow the capitalist system and take control themselves. Only then would a peaceful, harmonious society be possible.

There is an apocalyptic note of urgency about the *Manifesto*. Marx, Engels, and their comrades in the Communist League were convinced that the day of reckoning was close at hand. They believed that capitalism was in its death throes and that the working class needed a document explaining to them both why and how—though they were less clear on this—to finish it off.

Boils and Debt: How the *Manifesto* Was Written

Unfortunately for the revolution, Marx's sense of urgency seemed to evaporate once he was back in Belgium after the second congress of the Communist League. In the weeks after the congress, he appeared to do everything else— writing articles for other newspapers, giving lectures to workers' associations, traveling to Ghent to set up a local branch—but actually get down to the business in hand.

Finally, in frustration at his lack of action, the London leaders of the Communist League—Schapper, Bauer, and Moll—dispatched an ultimatum to Brussels on January 24, 1848. They declared that if the *Manifesto* did not reach London by February 1 of the current year, "further measures will have to be taken against him." If "Citizen Marx" could not fulfill his task, "the Central Committee requests the

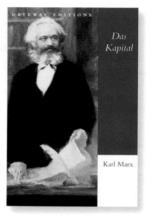

Marx's great work—so great that it is always known by its original name in German—*Das Kapital*. This was the study that put theoretical flesh on the bones sketched out originally in the *Manifesto*.

immediate return of the documents placed at his disposal." Karl Marx came very close to being taken off the job.

What were these documents? Marx probably had before him a draft from Schapper and Moll, possibly the rejected draft from Hess, and almost certainly notes from Engels. It is doubtful whether he did more than glance at the first two sets of documents. From the letters that passed between Marx and Engels at the time, it is clear that they had decided not to be bound by the instructions Marx had been given by the London committee.

The final warning seems to have spurred Marx into action. Fueled by coffee, brandy, and cigars, he scribbled furiously through the night in his study at 42 rue d'Orléans in Brussels. The text was produced on time. Writing 12,000 words in six weeks was no mean feat for a man who often suffered from serious apathy or an attack of boils when up against a deadline. This was, after all, the author who was confidently to predict some years later that he had only a few weeks' work left on Volume 1 of *Das Kapital*—a decade before he actually completed the book.

Engels always insisted that the main ideas of the *Manifesto* came from Marx. It is certainly true that the largest portion of credit—both for the substance and the composition—belongs to Marx, despite the fact that both names appear on the cover, at least of every modern edition. But Engels's fingerprints are all over it. The language of the final version still has the feel of the catechism, the question-and-answer format of Engels's original draft. These were abstract concepts expressed in clear language for a mass audience—something Engels was particularly good at. And many of the ideas in the *Manifesto* are found in *The German Ideology*, a book written by both men in 1845–46 for which they could not find a publisher.

When the *Manifesto* was published, Marx was 29 and Engels 27, and this was young men's work. It was ambitious, far-reaching, and enthusiastic, not stinting in its crushing demolition of rivals for the soul of communism— reforming socialists such as Pierre Proudhon in France and Robert Owen in Britain. It was also the clearest and most popular statement of Marx's beliefs that he ever managed.

Marx divided the *Manifesto* into four sections. Comparing them, it is immediately obvious that he was working against a difficult deadline. The first section contains a long recasting of history, whereas subsequent sections become more abbreviated and less considered, ending in the few, spluttered paragraphs of the fourth. And although the later sections are of interest to students of Marxism, it is the first section that makes the revolutionary aspects of the *Manifesto*—in both senses—immediately clear.

The two authors set out their theory of history right at the beginning, making it apparent that it is driven by a continuing conflict between those who control production and those who simply do the work. There are two hostile camps, they wrote, and never before in history have the bourgeoisie and the proletariat been so polarized. Marx and Engels then set out a great passage praising the bourgeoisie

The first page of the first edition of the first volume of *Das Kapital*, which was published in Hamburg in 1867.

for their own dramatic revolution against the forces of feudalism. By reducing everything to money, neither aristocracy, nor the church, nor the ancient forces of privilege can stand against them.

But the moment of crisis was fast approaching, the *Manifesto* explained. The lower middle class was being undermined by capitalist monopolies, the peasants were being forced off the land, and all the complex subtleties of class were being subsumed into the proletariat. Once they were aware of themselves, and of their power, it was inevitable that the proletariat would take power for themselves and usher in the communist age.

This was not a sentimental or ethical demand for changed working conditions—well into the twentieth century Marxists would condemn such reforms as obscuring the underlying class war. It was a call to arms, and a simple statement of the inevitability of the outcome. Like many historians and philosophers of the nineteenth century, Marx and Engels believed in the inevitable evolution of history: they just differed about where that evolution was leading.

In the second section of the *Manifesto*, the authors argued that communists were not opposed to other working-class parties, but they were deliberately international and they understood the historical significance of the proletariat—which rival parties might not. They then dealt with the four main objections to communism: the accusations that communists would do away with property rightfully earned; that they would introduce free love; that they would do away with the family; and that they would abolish nations and nationality. For all of these they turned the debate on its head, arguing that capitalism was producing all these situations anyway. They then rather undermined their great breadth of ambition with a modest and unambitious ten-point program for "most advanced countries"—the only practical description of what communism might be like.

The third section sets out the party's position against other socialist claimants, and the fourth section simply establishes who they support in which country.

The whole *Manifesto*, taken together, is broad, thrilling, angry, and refreshing. It is also completely ambiguous about the nature of the revolution, the vision of communism, the methods required before and after, and what the whole thing might mean in practice: a serious omission whose effects are now all too obvious.

Even Marx may have been aware that communism in practice might not have been to his taste. A friend once suggested that she could not imagine Marx living contentedly in an egalitarian society. "Neither can I," he agreed. "These times will come, but we must be away by then."

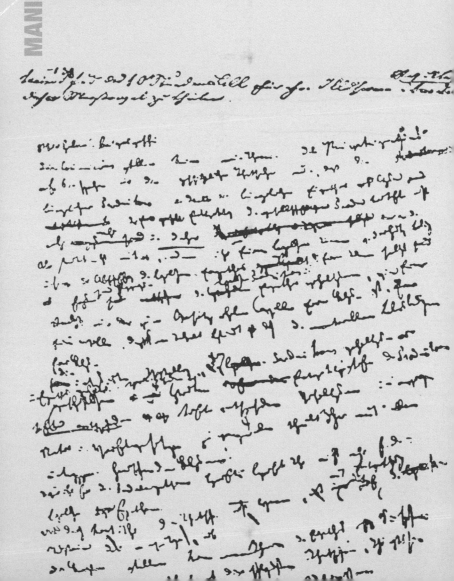

Manifesto of the Communist Party

A specter is haunting Europe—the specter of communism. All the powers of old Europe have entered into a holy alliance to exorcise this specter: Pope and Tsar, Metternich and Guizot, French Radicals, and German police-spies.

Where is the party in opposition that has not been decried as communistic by its opponents in power? Where is the opposition that has not hurled back the branding reproach of communism, against the more advanced opposition parties, as well as against its reactionary adversaries?

Two things result from this fact:

I. Communism is already acknowledged by all European powers to be itself a power.

II. It is high time that Communists should openly, in the face of the whole world, publish their views, their aims, their tendencies, and meet this nursery tale of the specter of communism with a manifesto of the party itself.

To this end, Communists of various nationalities have assembled in London and sketched the following manifesto, to be published in the English, French, German, Italian, Flemish, and Danish languages.

The first draft of the *Communist Manifesto*. It was purposely kept short and pithy, as Engels and Marx did not want their radical new political theory to be "confined in large tomes exclusively to the 'learned' world."

Bourgeois and Proletarians[1]

The history of all hitherto existing society[2] is the history of class struggles.

Freeman and slave, patrician and plebeian, lord and serf, guild-master[3] and journeyman, in a word, oppressor and oppressed, stood in constant opposition to one another, carried on an uninterrupted, now hidden, now open fight, a fight that each time ended, either in a revolutionary reconstitution of society at large, or in the common ruin of the contending classes.

In the earlier epochs of history, we find almost everywhere a complicated arrangement of society into various orders, a manifold gradation of social rank. In ancient Rome we have patricians, knights, plebeians, slaves; in the Middle Ages, feudal lords, vassals, guild-masters, journeymen, apprentices, serfs; in almost all of these classes, again, subordinate gradations.

The modern bourgeois society that has sprouted from the ruins of feudal society has not done away with class antagonisms. It has but established new classes, new conditions of oppression, new forms of struggle in place of the old ones.

Our epoch, the epoch of the bourgeoisie, possesses, however, this distinct feature: it has simplified class antagonisms. Society as a whole is more and more splitting up into two great hostile camps, into two great classes directly facing each other—bourgeoisie and proletariat.

From the serfs of the Middle Ages sprang the chartered burghers of the earliest towns. From these burgesses the first elements of the bourgeoisie were developed.

The discovery of America, the rounding of the Cape, opened up fresh ground for the rising bourgeoisie. The East-Indian and Chinese markets, the colonization of America, trade with the colonies, the increase in the means of exchange and in commodities generally, gave to commerce, to navigation, to industry, an impulse never before known, and thereby, to the revolutionary element in the tottering feudal society, a rapid development.

The feudal system of industry, in which industrial production was monopolized by closed guilds, now no longer suffices for the growing wants of the new markets. The manufacturing system took its place. The guild-masters were pushed aside by the manufacturing middle class; division of labor between the different corporate guilds vanished in the face of division of labor in each single workshop.

Meantime, the markets kept ever growing, the demand ever rising. Even manufacturers no longer sufficed. Thereupon, steam and machinery revolutionized industrial production. The place of manufacture was taken by the giant, Modern Industry; the place of the industrial middle class by industrial millionaires, the leaders of the whole industrial armies, the modern bourgeois.

Modern industry has established the world market, for which the discovery of America paved the way. This market has given an immense development to commerce, to navigation, to communication by land. This development has, in turn, reacted on the extension of industry; and in proportion as industry, commerce, navigation, railroads extended, in the same proportion the bourgeoisie developed, increased its capital, and pushed into the background every class handed down from the Middle Ages.

We see, therefore, how the modern bourgeoisie is itself the product of a long course of development, of a series of revolutions in the modes of production and of exchange.

Each step in the development of the bourgeoisie was accompanied by a corresponding political advance in that class. An oppressed class under the sway of the feudal nobility, an armed and self-governing association of medieval commune[4]: here independent urban republic (as in Italy and Germany); there taxable "third estate" of the monarchy (as in France); afterward, in the period of manufacturing proper, serving either the semifeudal or the absolute monarchy as a counterpoise against the nobility, and, in fact, cornerstone of the great monarchies in general—the bourgeoisie has at last, since the establishment of Modern

Industry and of the world market, conquered for itself, in the modern representative state, exclusive political sway. The executive of the modern state is but a committee for managing the common affairs of the whole bourgeoisie.

The bourgeoisie, historically, has played a most revolutionary part.

The bourgeoisie, wherever it has got the upper hand, has put an end to all feudal, patriarchal, idyllic relations. It has pitilessly torn asunder the motley feudal ties that bound man to his "natural superiors," and has left no other nexus between man and man than naked self-interest, than callous "cash payment." It has drowned out the most heavenly ecstasies of religious fervor, of chivalrous enthusiasm, of philistine sentimentalism, in the icy water of egotistical calculation. It has resolved personal worth into exchange value, and in place of the numberless indefeasible chartered freedoms, has set up that single, unconscionable freedom—Free Trade. In one word, for exploitation, veiled by religious and political illusions, it has substituted naked, shameless, direct, brutal exploitation.

The bourgeoisie has stripped of its halo every occupation hitherto honored and looked up to with reverent awe. It has converted the physician, the lawyer, the priest, the poet, the man of science, into its paid wage laborers.

The bourgeoisie has torn away from the family its sentimental veil, and has reduced the family relation into a mere money relation.

The bourgeoisie has disclosed how it came to pass that the brutal display of vigor in the Middle Ages, which reactionaries so much admire, found its fitting complement in the most slothful indolence. It has been the first to show what man's activity can bring about. It has accomplished wonders far surpassing Egyptian pyramids, Roman aqueducts, and Gothic cathedrals; it has conducted expeditions that put in the shade all former exoduses of nations and crusades.

The bourgeoisie cannot exist without constantly revolutionizing the instruments of production, and thereby the relations of production, and with them the whole relations of society. Conservation of the old modes of production in unaltered form, was, on the contrary, the first condition of existence for all earlier industrial classes. Constant revolutionizing of production, uninterrupted disturbance of all social conditions, everlasting uncertainty, and agitation distinguish the bourgeois epoch from all earlier ones. All fixed, fast-frozen relations, with their train of ancient and venerable prejudices and opinions, are swept away, all new-formed ones become antiquated before they can ossify. All that is solid melts into air, all that is holy is profaned, and man is at last compelled to face with sober senses his real condition of life and his relations with his kind.

The need of a constantly expanding market for its products chases the bourgeoisie over the entire surface of the globe. It must nestle everywhere, settle everywhere, establish connections everywhere.

The bourgeoisie has, through its exploitation of the world market, given a cosmopolitan character to production and consumption in every country. To the great chagrin of reactionaries, it has drawn from under the feet of industry the national ground on which it stood. All old-established national industries have been destroyed or are daily being destroyed. They are dislodged by new industries, whose introduction becomes a life and death question for all civilized nations, by industries that no longer work up indigenous raw material, but raw material drawn from the remotest zones; industries whose products are consumed, not only at home, but in every quarter of the globe. In place of the old wants, satisfied by the production of the country, we find new wants, requiring for their satisfaction the products of distant lands and climes. In place of the old local and national seclusion and self-sufficiency, we have intercourse in every direction, universal interdependence of nations.

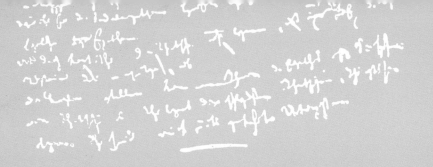

And as in material, so also in intellectual production. The intellectual creations of individual nations become common property. National one-sidedness and narrow-mindedness become more and more impossible, and from the numerous national and local literatures, there arises a world literature.

The bourgeoisie, by the rapid improvement of all instruments of production, by the immensely facilitated means of communication, draws all, even the most barbarian, nations into civilization. The cheap prices of commodities are the heavy artillery, with which it batters down all Chinese walls, with which it forces the barbarians' intensely obstinate hatred of foreigners to capitulate. It compels all nations, on pain of extinction, to adopt the bourgeois mode of production; it compels them to introduce what it calls civilization into their midst, i.e., to become bourgeois themselves. In one word, it creates a world after its own image.

The bourgeoisie has subjected the country to the rule of the towns. It has created enormous cities, has greatly increased the urban population as compared with the rural, and has thus rescued a considerable part of the population from the idiocy of rural life. Just as it has made the country dependent on the towns, so it has made barbarian and semibarbarian countries dependent on the civilized ones, nations of peasants on nations of bourgeois, the East on the West.

The bourgeoisie keeps more and more doing away with the scattered state of the population, of the means of production, and of property. It has agglomerated population, centralized the means of production, and has concentrated property in a few hands. The necessary consequence of this was political centralization. Independent, or but loosely connected provinces, with separate interests, laws, governments, and systems of taxation, became lumped together into one nation, with one government, one code of laws, one national class interest, one frontier, and one customs tariff.

The bourgeoisie, during its rule of scarce one hundred years, has created more massive and more colossal productive forces than have all preceding generations together. Subjection of nature's forces to man, machinery, application of chemistry to industry and agriculture, steam navigation, railroads, electric telegraphs, clearing of whole continents for cultivation, canalization of rivers, whole populations conjured out of the ground—what earlier century had even a presentiment that such productive forces slumbered in the lap of social labor?

We see then: the means of production and of exchange, on whose foundation the bourgeoisie built itself up, were generated in feudal society. At a certain stage in the development of these means of production and of exchange, the conditions under which feudal society produced and exchanged, the feudal organization of agriculture and manufacturing industry, in one word, the feudal relations of property became no longer compatible with the already developed productive forces; they became so many fetters. They had to be burst asunder; they were burst asunder.

Into their place stepped free competition, accompanied by a social and political constitution adapted in it, and the economic and political sway of the bourgeois class.

A similar movement is going on before our own eyes. Modern bourgeois society, with its relations of production, of exchange and of property, a society that has conjured up such gigantic means of production and of exchange, is like the sorcerer who is no longer able to control the powers of the nether world whom he has called up by his spells. For many a decade past, the history of industry and commerce is but the history of the revolt of modern productive forces against modern conditions of production, against the property relations that are the conditions for the existence of the bourgeois and of its rule. It is enough to mention the commercial crises that, by their periodical return, put the existence of the entire bourgeois society on its trial, each time more threateningly. In these crises, a great part not only of the existing products, but also of the previously created productive forces, are periodically destroyed. In these crises, there breaks out an epidemic that, in all earlier epochs, would have seemed an absurdity—the epidemic of overproduction. Society suddenly finds itself put back into a state of momentary barbarism; it appears as if a famine, a universal war of

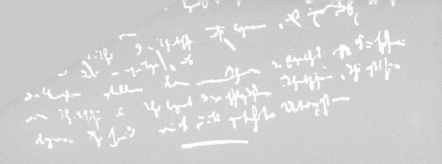

devastation, had cut off the supply of every means of subsistence; industry and commerce seem to be destroyed. And why? Because there is too much civilization, too much means of subsistence, too much industry, too much commerce. The productive forces at the disposal of society no longer tend to further the development of the conditions of bourgeois property; on the contrary, they have become too powerful for these conditions, by which they are fettered, and so soon as they overcome these fetters, they bring disorder into the whole of bourgeois society, endanger the existence of bourgeois property. The conditions of bourgeois society are too narrow to comprise the wealth created by them. And how does the bourgeoisie get over these crises? On the one hand, by enforced destruction of a mass of productive forces; on the other, by the conquest of new markets, and by the more thorough exploitation of the old ones. That is to say, by paving the way for more extensive and more destructive crises, and by diminishing the means whereby crises are prevented.

The weapons with which the bourgeoisie felled feudalism to the ground are now turned against the bourgeoisie itself.

But not only has the bourgeoisie forged the weapons that bring death to itself; it has also called into existence the men who are to wield those weapons—the modern working class— the proletarians.

In proportion as the bourgeoisie, i.e., capital, is developed, in the same proportion is the proletariat, the modern working class, developed—a class of laborers, who live only so long as they find work, and who find work only so long as their labor increases capital. These laborers, who must sell themselves piecemeal, are a commodity, like every other article of commerce, and are consequently exposed to all the vicissitudes of competition, to all the fluctuations of the market.

Owing to the extensive use of machinery, and to the division of labor, the work of the proletarians has lost all individual character, and, consequently, all charm for the workman. He becomes an appendage of the machine, and it is only the most simple, most monotonous, and most easily acquired knack, that is required of him. Hence, the cost of production of a workman is restricted, almost entirely, to the means of subsistence that he requires for maintenance, and for the propagation of his race. But the price of a commodity, and therefore also of labor, is equal to its cost of production. In proportion, therefore, as the repulsiveness of the work increases, the wage decreases. What is more, in proportion as the use of machinery and division of labor increases, in the same proportion the burden of toil also increases, whether by prolongation of the working hours, by the increase of the work exacted in a given time, or by increased speed of machinery, etc.

Modern Industry has converted the little workshop of the patriarchal master into the great factory of the industrial capitalist. Masses of laborers, crowded into the factory, are organized like soldiers. As privates of the industrial army, they are placed under the command of a perfect hierarchy of officers and sergeants. Not only are they slaves of the bourgeois class, and of the bourgeois state; they are daily and hourly enslaved by the machine, by the overlooker, and, above all, by the individual bourgeois manufacturer himself. The more openly this despotism proclaims gain to be its end and aim, the more petty, the more hateful, and the more embittering it is.

The less the skill and exertion of strength implied in manual labor, in other words, the more modern industry becomes developed, the more is the labor of men superseded by that of women. Differences of age and sex have no longer any distinctive social validity for the working class. All are instruments of labor, more or less expensive to use, according to their age and sex.

No sooner is the exploitation of the laborer by the manufacturer, so far at an end, that he receives his wages in cash, than he is set upon by the other portion of the bourgeoisie, the landlord, the shopkeeper, the pawnbroker, etc.

The lower strata of the middle class—the small tradespeople, shopkeepers, and retired tradesmen generally, the handicraftsmen and peasants—all these sink gradually into the

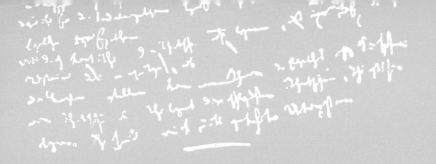

proletariat, partly because their diminutive capital does not suffice for the scale on which Modern Industry is carried on, and is swamped in the competition with the large capitalists, partly because their specialized skill is rendered worthless by new methods of production. Thus, the proletariat is recruited from all classes of the population.

The proletariat goes through various stages of development. With its birth begins its struggle with the bourgeoisie. At first, the contest is carried on by individual laborers, then by the work of people of a factory, then by the operative of one trade, in one locality, against the individual bourgeois who directly exploits them. They direct their attacks not against the bourgeois condition of production, but against the instruments of production themselves; they destroy imported wares that compete with their labor, they smash to pieces machinery, they set factories ablaze, they seek to restore by force the vanished status of the workman of the Middle Ages.

At this stage, the laborers still form an incoherent mass scattered over the whole country, and broken up by their mutual competition. If anywhere they unite to form more compact bodies, this is not yet the consequence of their own active union, but of the union of the bourgeoisie, which, in order to attain its own political ends, is compelled to set the whole proletariat in motion, and is moreover yet, for a time, able to do so. At this stage, therefore, the proletarians do not fight their enemies, but the enemies of their enemies, the remnants of absolute monarchy, the landowners, the nonindustrial bourgeois, the petty bourgeois. Thus, the whole historical movement is concentrated in the hands of the bourgeoisie; every victory so obtained is a victory for the bourgeoisie.

But with the development of industry, the proletariat not only increases in number; it becomes concentrated in greater masses, its strength grows, and it feels that strength more. The various interests and conditions of life within the ranks of the proletariat are more and more equalized, in proportion as machinery obliterates all distinctions of labor, and nearly everywhere reduces wages to the same low level. The growing competition among the bourgeois, and the resulting commercial crises, make the wages of the workers ever more fluctuating. The increasing improvement of machinery, ever more rapidly developing, makes their livelihood more and more precarious; the collisions between individual workmen and individual bourgeois take more and more the character of collisions between two classes. Thereupon, the workers begin to form combinations (trade unions) against the bourgeois; they club together in order to keep up the rate of wages; they found permanent associations in order to make provision beforehand for these occasional revolts. Here and there, the contest breaks out into riots.

Now and then the workers are victorious, but only for a time. The real fruit of their battles lie not in the immediate result, but in the ever expanding union of the workers. This union is helped on by the improved means of communication that are created by Modern Industry, and that place the workers of different localities in contact with one another. It was just this contact that was needed to centralize the numerous local struggles, all of the same character, into one national struggle between classes. But every class struggle is a political struggle. And that union, to attain which the burghers of the Middle Ages, with their miserable highways, required centuries, the modern proletarians, thanks to railroads, achieve in a few years.

This organization of the proletarians into a class, and, consequently, into a political party, is continually being upset again by the competition between the workers themselves. But it ever rises up again, stronger, firmer, mightier. It compels legislative recognition of particular interests of the workers, by taking advantage of the divisions among the bourgeoisie itself. Thus, the Ten-Hours Bill in England was carried.

Altogether, collisions between the classes of the old society further in many ways the course of development of the proletariat. The bourgeoisie finds itself involved in a constant battle. At first with the aristocracy; later on, with those portions of the bourgeoisie itself, whose interests have become antagonistic to the progress of industry; at all time with the

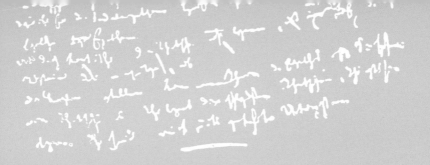

bourgeoisie of foreign countries. In all these battles, it sees itself compelled to appeal to the proletariat, to ask for help, and thus to drag it into the political arena. The bourgeoisie itself, therefore, supplies the proletariat with its own elements of political and general education, in other words, it furnishes the proletariat with weapons for fighting the bourgeoisie.

Further, as we have already seen, entire sections of the ruling class are, by the advance of industry, precipitated into the proletariat, or are at least threatened in their conditions of existence. These also supply the proletariat with fresh elements of enlightenment and progress.

Finally, in times when the class struggle nears the decisive hour, the progress of dissolution going on within the ruling class, in fact within the whole range of old society, assumes such a violent, glaring character, that a small section of the ruling class cuts itself adrift, and joins the revolutionary class, the class that holds the future in its hands. Just as, therefore, at an earlier period, a section of the nobility went over to the bourgeoisie, so now a portion of the bourgeoisie goes over to the proletariat, and in particular, a portion of the bourgeois ideologists, who have raised themselves to the level of comprehending theoretically the historical movement as a whole.

Of all the classes that stand face to face with the bourgeoisie today, the proletariat alone is a genuinely revolutionary class. The other classes decay and finally disappear in the face of Modern Industry; the proletariat is its special and essential product.

The lower middle class, the small manufacturer, the shopkeeper, the artisan, the peasant, all these fight against the bourgeoisie, to save from extinction their existence as fractions of the middle class. They are therefore not revolutionary, but conservative. Nay, more, they are reactionary, for they try to roll back the wheel of history. If, by chance, they are revolutionary, they are only so in view of their impending transfer into the proletariat; they thus defend not their present, but their future interests; they desert their own standpoint to place themselves at that of the proletariat.

The "dangerous class," the social scum, that passively rotting mass thrown off by the lowest layers of the old society, may, here and there, be swept into the movement by a proletarian revolution; its conditions of life, however, prepare it far more for the part of a bribed tool of reactionary intrigue.

In the condition of the proletariat, those of old society at large are already virtually swamped. The proletarian is without property; his relation to his wife and children has no longer anything in common with the bourgeois family relations; modern industry labor, modern subjection to capital, the same in England as in France, in America as in Germany, has stripped him of every trace of national character. Law, morality, religion, are to him so many bourgeois prejudices, behind which lurk in ambush just as many bourgeois interests.

All the preceding classes that got the upper hand sought to fortify their already acquired status by subjecting society at large to their conditions of appropriation. The proletarians cannot become masters of the productive forces of society, except by abolishing their own previous mode of appropriation, and thereby also every other previous mode of appropriation. They have nothing of their own to secure and to fortify; their mission is to destroy all previous securities for, and insurances of, individual property.

All previous historical movements were movements of minorities, or in the interest of minorities. The proletarian movement is the self-conscious, independent movement of the immense majority, in the interest of the immense majority. The proletariat, the lowest stratum of our present society, cannot stir, cannot raise itself up, without the whole super incumbent strata of official society being sprung into the air.

Though not in substance, yet in form, the struggle of the proletariat with the bourgeoisie is at first a national struggle. The proletariat of each country must, of course, first of all settle matters with its own bourgeoisie.

In depicting the most general phases of the development of the proletariat, we traced the more or less veiled civil war, raging within existing society, up to the point where that war breaks out into open revolution, and where the violent overthrow of the bourgeoisie lays the foundation for the sway of the proletariat.

Hitherto, every form of society has been based, as we have already seen, on the antagonism of oppressing and oppressed classes. But in order to oppress a class, certain conditions must be assured to it under which it can, at least, continue its slavish existence. The serf, in the period of serfdom, raised himself to membership in the commune, just as the petty bourgeois, under the yoke of the feudal absolutism, managed to develop into a bourgeois. The modern laborer, on the contrary, instead of rising with the process of industry, sinks deeper and deeper below the conditions of existence of his own class. He becomes a pauper, and pauperism develops more rapidly than population and wealth. And here it becomes evident that the bourgeoisie is unfit any longer to be the ruling class in society, and to impose its conditions of existence upon society as an overriding law. It is unfit to rule because it is incompetent to assure an existence to its slave within his slavery, because it cannot help letting him sink into such a state, that it has to feed him, instead of being fed by him. Society can no longer live under this bourgeoisie, in other words, its existence is no longer compatible with society.

The essential conditions for the existence and for the sway of the bourgeois class is the formation and augmentation of capital; the condition for capital is wage labor. Wage labor rests exclusively on competition between the laborers. The advance of industry, whose involuntary promoter is the bourgeoisie, replaces the isolation of the laborers, due to competition, by the revolutionary combination, due to association. The development of Modern Industry, therefore, cuts from under its feet the very foundation on which the bourgeoisie produces and appropriates products. What the bourgeoisie therefore produces, above all, are its own grave-diggers. Its fall and the victory of the proletariat are equally inevitable.

Proletarians and Communists

In what relation do the Communists stand to the proletarians as a whole? The Communists do not form a separate party opposed to the other working-class parties.

They have no interests separate and apart from those of the proletariat as a whole.

They do not set up any sectarian principles of their own, by which to shape and mold the proletarian movement.

The Communists are distinguished from the other working-class parties by this only:

> (1) In the national struggles of the proletarians of the different countries, they point out and bring to the front the common interests of the entire proletariat, independently of all nationality.

> (2) In the various stages of development which the struggle of the working class against the bourgeoisie has to pass through, they always and everywhere represent the interests of the movement as a whole.

The Communists, therefore, are on the one hand, practically, the most advanced and resolute section of the working-class parties of every country, that section which pushes forward all others; on the other hand, theoretically, they have over the great mass of the proletariat the advantage of clearly understanding the lines of march, the conditions, and the ultimate general results of the proletarian movement.

The immediate aim of the Communists is the same as that of all other proletarian parties: Formation of the proletariat into a class, overthrow of the bourgeois supremacy, conquest of political power by the proletariat.

The theoretical conclusions of the Communists are in no way based on ideas or principles that have been invented, or discovered, by this or that would-be universal reformer.

They merely express, in general terms, actual relations springing from an existing class struggle, from a historical movement going on under our very eyes. The abolition of existing property relations is not at all a distinctive feature of communism.

All property relations in the past have continually been subject to historical change consequent upon the change in historical conditions.

The French Revolution, for example, abolished feudal property in favor of bourgeois property.

The distinguishing feature of communism is not the abolition of property generally, but the abolition of bourgeois property. But modern bourgeois private property is the final and most complete expression of the system of producing and appropriating products that is based on class antagonisms, on the exploitation of the many by the few.

In this sense, the theory of the Communists may be summed up in the single sentence: Abolition of private property.

We Communists have been reproached with the desire of abolishing the right of personally acquiring property as the fruit of a man's own labor, which property is alleged to be the groundwork of all personal freedom, activity, and independence.

Hard-won, self-acquired, self-earned property! Do you mean the property of petty artisan and of the small peasant, a form of property that preceded the bourgeois form? There is no need to abolish that; the development of industry has to a great extent already destroyed it, and is still destroying it daily.

Or do you mean the modern bourgeois private property?

But does wage labor create any property for the laborer? Not a bit. It creates capital, i.e., that kind of property which exploits wage labor, and which cannot increase except upon conditions of begetting a new supply of wage labor for fresh exploitation. Property, in its present form, is based on the antagonism of capital and wage labor. Let us examine both sides of this antagonism.

To be a capitalist, is to have not only a purely personal, but a social status in production. Capital is a collective product, and only by the united action of many members, nay, in the last resort, only by the united action of all members of society, can it be set in motion.

Capital is therefore not only personal; it is a social power.

When, therefore, capital is converted into common property, into the property of all members of society, personal property is not thereby transformed into social property. It is only the social character of the property that is changed. It loses its class character.

Let us now take wage labor.

The average price of wage labor is the minimum wage, i.e., that quantum of the means of subsistence which is absolutely requisite to keep the laborer in bare existence as a laborer. What, therefore, the wage laborer appropriates by means of his labor merely suffices to prolong and reproduce a bare existence. We by no means intend to abolish this personal appropriation of the products of labor, an appropriation that is made for the maintenance and reproduction of human life, and that leaves no surplus wherewith to command the labor of others. All that we want to do away with is the miserable character of this appropriation, under which the laborer lives merely to increase capital, and is allowed to live only in so far as the interest of the ruling class requires it.

In bourgeois society, living labor is but a means to increase accumulated labor. In communist society, accumulated labor is but a means to widen, to enrich, to promote the existence of the laborer.

In bourgeois society, therefore, the past dominates the present; in communist society, the present dominates the past. In bourgeois society, capital is independent and has individuality, while the living person is dependent and has no individuality.

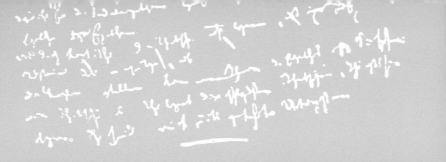

And the abolition of this state of things is called by the bourgeois, abolition of individuality and freedom! And rightly so. The abolition of bourgeois individuality, bourgeois independence, and bourgeois freedom is undoubtedly aimed at.

By freedom is meant, under the present bourgeois conditions of production, free trade, free selling and buying.

But if selling and buying disappears, free selling and buying disappears also. This talk about free selling and buying, and all the other "brave words" of our bourgeois about freedom in general, have a meaning, if any, only in contrast with restricted selling and buying, with the fettered traders of the Middle Ages, but have no meaning when opposed to the communist abolition of buying and selling, or the bourgeois conditions of production, and of the bourgeoisie itself.

You are horrified at our intending to do away with private property. But in your existing society, private property is already done away with for nine-tenths of the population; its existence for the few is solely due to its nonexistence in the hands of those nine-tenths. You reproach us, therefore, with intending to do away with a form of property, the necessary condition for whose existence is the nonexistence of any property for the immense majority of society.

In one word, you reproach us with intending to do away with your property. Precisely so; that is just what we intend.

From the moment when labor can no longer be converted into capital, money, or rent, into a social power capable of being monopolized, i.e., from the moment when individual property can no longer be transformed into bourgeois property, into capital, from that moment, you say, individuality vanishes.

You must, therefore, confess that by "individual" you mean no other person than the bourgeois, than the middle-class owner of property. This person must, indeed, be swept out of the way, and made impossible.

Communism deprives no man of the power to appropriate the products of society; all that it does is to deprive him of the power to subjugate the labor of others by means of such appropriations.

It has been objected that upon the abolition of private property, all work will cease, and universal laziness will overtake us.

According to this, bourgeois society ought long ago to have gone to the dogs through sheer idleness; for those who acquire anything, do not work. The whole of this objection is but another expression of the tautology: There can no longer be any wage labor when there is no longer any capital.

All objections urged against the communistic mode of producing and appropriating material products, have, in the same way, been urged against the communistic mode of producing and appropriating intellectual products. Just as to the bourgeois, the disappearance of class property is the disappearance of production itself, so the disappearance of class culture is to him identical with the disappearance of all culture.

That culture, the loss of which he laments, is, for the enormous majority, a mere training to act as a machine.

But don't wrangle with us so long as you apply, to our intended abolition of bourgeois property, the standard of your bourgeois notions of freedom, culture, law, etc. Your very ideas are but the outgrowth of the conditions of your bourgeois production and bourgeois property, just as your jurisprudence is but the will of your class made into a law for all, a will whose essential character and direction are determined by the economical conditions of existence of your class.

The selfish misconception that induces you to transform into eternal laws of nature and of reason the social forms stringing from your present mode of production and form of property—historical relations that rise and disappear in the progress of production—this

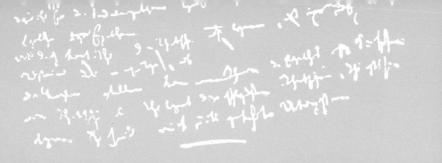

misconception you share with every ruling class that has preceded you. What you see clearly in the case of ancient property, what you admit in the case of feudal property, you are of course forbidden to admit in the case of your own bourgeois form of property.

Abolition of the family! Even the most radical flare up at this infamous proposal of the Communists.

On what foundation is the present family, the bourgeois family, based? On capital, on private gain. In its completely developed form, this family exists only among the bourgeoisie. But this state of things finds its complement in the practical absence of the family among proletarians, and in public prostitution.

The bourgeois family will vanish as a matter of course when its complement vanishes, and both will vanish with the vanishing of capital.

Do you charge us with wanting to stop the exploitation of children by their parents? To this crime we plead guilty.

But, you say, we destroy the most hallowed of relations, when we replace home education by social.

And your education! Is not that also social, and determined by the social conditions under which you educate, by the intervention direct or indirect, of society, by means of schools, etc.? The Communists have not intended the intervention of society in education; they do but seek to alter the character of that intervention, and to rescue education from the influence of the ruling class.

The bourgeois claptrap about the family and education, about the hallowed correlation of parents and child, becomes all the more disgusting, the more, by the action of Modern Industry, all the family ties among the proletarians are torn asunder, and their children transformed into simple articles of commerce and instruments of labor.

But you Communists would introduce community of women, screams the bourgeoisie in chorus.

The bourgeois sees his wife a mere instrument of production. He hears that the instruments of production are to be exploited in common, and, naturally, can come to no other conclusion that the lot of being common to all will likewise fall to the women.

He has not even a suspicion that the real point aimed at is to do away with the status of women as mere instruments of production.

For the rest, nothing is more ridiculous than the virtuous indignation of our bourgeois at the community of women which, they pretend, is to be openly and officially established by the Communists. The Communists have no need to introduce free love; it has existed almost from time immemorial.

Our bourgeois, not content with having wives and daughters of their proletarians at their disposal, not to speak of common prostitutes, take the greatest pleasure in seducing each other's wives.

Bourgeois marriage is, in reality, a system of wives in common and thus, at the most, what the Communists might possibly be reproached with is that they desire to introduce, in substitution for a hypocritically concealed, an openly legalized system of free love. For the rest, it is self-evident that the abolition of the present system of production must bring with it the abolition of free love springing from that system, i.e., of prostitution both public and private.

The Communists are further reproached with desiring to abolish countries and nationality.

The working men have no country. We cannot take from them what they have not got. Since the proletariat must first of all acquire political supremacy, must rise to be the leading class of the nation, must constitute itself the nation, it is, so far, itself national, though not in the bourgeois sense of the word.

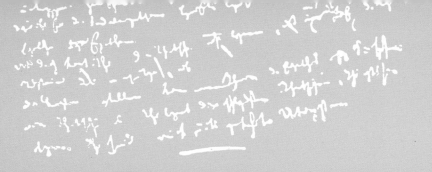

National differences and antagonism between peoples are daily more and more vanishing, owing to the development of the bourgeoisie, to freedom of commerce, to the world market, to uniformity in the mode of production and in the conditions of life corresponding thereto.

The supremacy of the proletariat will cause them to vanish still faster. United action of the leading civilized countries at least is one of the first conditions for the emancipation of the proletariat.

In proportion as the exploitation of one individual by another will also be put an end to, the exploitation of one nation by another will also be put an end to. In proportion as the antagonism between classes within the nation vanishes, the hostility of one nation to another will come to an end.

The charges against communism made from a religious, a philosophical, and, generally, from an ideological standpoint, are not deserving of serious examination.

Does it require deep intuition to comprehend that man's ideas, views, and conception, in one word, man's consciousness, changes with every change in the conditions of his material existence, in his social relations, and in his social life?

What else does the history of ideas prove, than that intellectual production changes its character in proportion as material production is changed? The ruling ideas of each age have ever been the ideas of its ruling class.

When people speak of the ideas that revolutionize society, they do but express that fact that within the old society the elements of a new one have been created, and that the dissolution of the old ideas keeps even pace with the dissolution of the old conditions of existence.

When the ancient world was in its last throes, the ancient religions were overcome by Christianity. When Christian ideas succumbed in the eighteenth century to rationalist ideas, feudal society fought its death battle with the then revolutionary bourgeoisie. The ideas of religious liberty and freedom of conscience merely gave expression to the sway of free competition within the domain of knowledge.

"Undoubtedly," it will be said, "religious, moral, philosophical, and juridical ideas have been modified in the course of historical development. But religion, morality, philosophy, political science, and law, constantly survived this change."

"There are, besides, eternal truths, such as Freedom, Justice, etc., that are common to all states of society. But communism abolishes eternal truths, it abolishes all religion, and all morality, instead of constituting them on a new basis; it therefore acts in contradiction to all past historical experience."

What does this accusation reduce itself to? The history of all past society has consisted in the development of class antagonisms, antagonisms that assumed different forms at different epochs.

But whatever form they may have taken, one fact is common to all past ages, viz., the exploitation of one part of society by the other. No wonder, then, that the social consciousness of past ages, despite all the multiplicity and variety it displays, moves within certain common forms, or general ideas, which cannot completely vanish except with the total disappearance of class antagonisms.

The communist revolution is the most radical rupture with traditional relations; no wonder that its development involved the most radical rupture with traditional ideas.

But let us have done with the bourgeois objections to communism.

We have seen above that the first step in the revolution by the working class is to raise the proletariat to the position of ruling class to win the battle of democracy.

The proletariat will use its political supremacy to wrest, by degree, all capital from the bourgeoisie, to centralize all instruments of production in the hands of the state, i.e., of the proletariat organized as the ruling class; and to increase the total productive forces as rapidly as possible.

Of course, in the beginning, this cannot be effected except by means of despotic inroads on the rights of property, and on the conditions of bourgeois production; by means of measures, therefore, which appear economically insufficient and untenable, but which, in the course of the movement, outstrip themselves, necessitate further inroads upon the old social order, and are unavoidable as a means of entirely revolutionizing the mode of production.

These measures will, of course, be different in different countries.

Nevertheless, in most advanced countries, the following will be pretty generally applicable.

1. Abolition of property in land and application of all rents of land to public purposes.

2. A heavy progressive or graduated income tax.

3. Abolition of all rights of inheritance.

4. Confiscation of the property of all emigrants and rebels.

5. Centralization of credit in the banks of the state, by means of a national bank with state capital and an exclusive monopoly.

6. Centralization of the means of communication and transport in the hands of the state.

7. Extension of factories and instruments of production owned by the state; the bringing into cultivation of wastelands, and the improvement of the soil generally in accordance with a common plan.

8. Equal obligation of all to work. Establishment of industrial armies, especially for agriculture.

9. Combination of agriculture with manufacturing industries; gradual abolition of all the distinction between town and country by a more equable distribution of the populace over the country.

10. Free education for all children in public schools. Abolition of children's factory labor in its present form. Combination of education with industrial production, etc.

When, in the course of development, class distinctions have disappeared, and all production has been concentrated in the hands of a vast association of the whole nation, the public power will lose its political character. Political power, properly so called, is merely the organized power of one class for oppressing another. If the proletariat during its contest with the bourgeoisie is compelled, by the force of circumstances, to organize itself as a class; if, by means of a revolution, it makes itself the ruling class, and, as such, sweeps away by force the old conditions of production, then it will, along with these conditions, have swept away the conditions for the existence of class antagonisms and of classes generally, and will thereby have abolished its own supremacy as a class.

In place of the old bourgeois society, with its classes and class antagonisms, we shall have an association in which the free development of each is the condition for the free development of all.

Socialist and Communist Literature

1. Reactionary Socialism

A. Feudal Socialism

Owing to their historical position, it became the vocation of the aristocracies of France and England to write pamphlets against modern bourgeois society. In the French Revolution of July 1830, and in the English reform agitation, these aristocracies again succumbed to the hateful upstart. Thenceforth, a serious political struggle was altogether out of the question. A literary battle alone remained possible. But even in the domain of literature, the old cries of the restoration period had become impossible.[5]

In order to arouse sympathy, the aristocracy was obliged to lose sight, apparently, of its own interests, and to formulate its indictment against the bourgeoisie in the interest of the exploited working class alone. Thus, the aristocracy took their revenge by singing lampoons on their new masters and whispering in his ears sinister prophesies of coming catastrophe.

In this way arose feudal socialism: half lamentation, half lampoon; half an echo of the past, half menace of the future; at times, by its bitter, witty, and incisive criticism, striking the bourgeoisie to the very heart's core, but always ludicrous in its effect, through total incapacity to comprehend the march of modern history.

The aristocracy, in order to rally the people to them, waved the proletarian alms-bag in front for a banner. But the people, so often as it joined them, saw on their hindquarters the old feudal coats of arms, and deserted with loud and irreverent laughter.

One section of the French Legitimists and "Young England" exhibited this spectacle.

In pointing out that their mode of exploitation was different to that of the bourgeoisie, the feudalists forget that they exploited under circumstances and conditions that were quite different and that are now antiquated. In showing that, under their rule, the modern proletariat never existed, they forget that the modern bourgeoisie is the necessary offspring of their own form of society.

For the rest, so little do they conceal the reactionary character of their criticism that their chief accusation against the bourgeois amounts to this: that under the bourgeois regime a class is being developed which is destined to cut up, root and branch, the old order of society.

What they upbraid the bourgeoisie with is not so much that it creates a proletariat as that it creates a revolutionary proletariat.

In political practice, therefore, they join in all corrective measures against the working class; and in ordinary life, despite their highfalutin phrases, they stoop to pick up the golden apples dropped from the tree of industry, and to barter truth, love, and honor, for traffic in wool, beetroot-sugar, and potato spirits.[6]

As the parson has ever gone hand in hand with the landlord, so has clerical socialism with feudal socialism.

Nothing is easier than to give Christian asceticism a socialist tinge. Has not Christianity declaimed against private property, against marriage, against the state? Has it not preached in the place of these, charity and poverty, celibacy and mortification of the flesh, monastic life and Mother Church? Christian socialism is but the holy water with which the priest consecrates the heart-burnings of the aristocrat.

B. Petty-Bourgeois Socialism

The feudal aristocracy was not the only class that was ruined by the bourgeoisie, not the only class whose conditions of existence pined and perished in the atmosphere of modern bourgeois society. The medieval burgesses and the small peasant proprietors were the precursors of the modern bourgeoisie. In those countries which are but little developed, industrially and commercially, these two classes still vegetate side by side with the rising bourgeoisie.

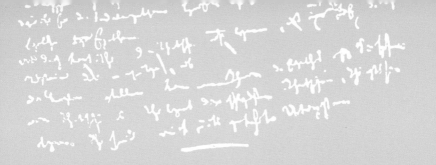

In countries where modern civilization has become fully developed, a new class of petty bourgeois has been formed, fluctuating between proletariat and bourgeoisie, and ever renewing itself a supplementary part of bourgeois society. The individual members of this class, however, as being constantly hurled down into the proletariat by the action of competition, and, as Modern Industry develops, they even see the moment approaching when they will completely disappear as an independent section of modern society, to be replaced in manufactures, agriculture, and commerce, by overlookers, bailiffs, and shopmen.

In countries like France, where the peasants constitute far more than half of the population, it was natural that writers who sided with the proletariat against the bourgeoisie should use, in their criticism of the bourgeois regime, the standard of the peasant and petty bourgeois, and from the standpoint of these intermediate classes, should take up the cudgels for the working class. Thus arose petty-bourgeois socialism. Sismondi was the head of this school, not only in France but also in England.

This school of socialism dissected with great acuteness the contradictions in the conditions of modern production. It laid bare the hypocritical apologies of economists. It proved, incontrovertibly, the disastrous effects of machinery and division of labor; the concentration of capital and land in a few hands; overproduction and crises; it pointed out the inevitable ruin of the petty bourgeois and peasant, the misery of the proletariat, the anarchy in production, the crying inequalities in the distribution of wealth, the industrial war of extermination between nations, the dissolution of old moral bonds, of the old family relations, of the old nationalities.

In it positive aims, however, this form of socialism aspires either to restoring the old means of production and of exchange, and with them the old property relations, and the old society, or to cramping the modern means of production and of exchange within the framework of the old property relations that have been, and were bound to be, exploded by those means. In either case, it is both reactionary and Utopian.

Its last words are: corporate guilds for manufacture; patriarchal relations in agriculture.

Ultimately, when stubborn historical facts had dispersed all intoxicating effects of self-deception, this form of socialism ended in a miserable hangover.

C. German or "True" Socialism

The socialist and communist literature of France, a literature that originated under the pressure of a bourgeoisie in power, and that was the expressions of the struggle against this power, was introduced into Germany at a time when the bourgeoisie in that country had just begun its contest with feudal absolutism.

German philosophers, would-be philosophers, and beaux esprits (men of letters), eagerly seized on this literature, only forgetting that when these writings immigrated from France into Germany, French social conditions had not immigrated along with them. In contact with German social conditions, this French literature lost all its immediate practical significance and assumed a purely literary aspect. Thus, to the German philosophers of the eighteenth century, the demands of the first French Revolution were nothing more than the demands of "Practical Reason" in general, and the utterance of the will of the revolutionary French bourgeoisie signified, in their eyes, the laws of pure will, of will as it was bound to be, of true human will generally.

The work of the German literati consisted solely in bringing the new French ideas into harmony with their ancient philosophical conscience, or rather, in annexing the French ideas without deserting their own philosophic point of view.

This annexation took place in the same way in which a foreign language is appropriated, namely, by translation.

It is well known how the monks wrote silly lives of Catholic saints over the manuscripts on which the classical works of ancient heathendom had been written. The German literati reversed this process with the profane French literature. They wrote their philosophical

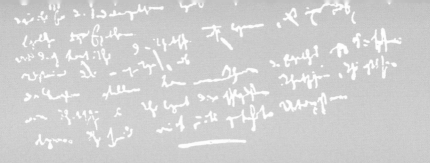

nonsense beneath the French original. For instance, beneath the French criticism of the economic functions of money, they wrote "alienation of humanity," and beneath the French criticism of the bourgeois state they wrote "dethronement of the category of the general," and so forth.

The introduction of these philosophical phrases at the back of the French historical criticisms, they dubbed "Philosophy of Action," "True Socialism," "German Science of Socialism," "Philosophical Foundation of Socialism," and so on.

The French socialist and communist literature was thus completely emasculated. And, since it ceased, in the hands of the German, to express the struggle of one class with the other, he felt conscious of having overcome "French one-sidedness" and of representing, not true requirements, but the requirements of truth; not the interests of the proletariat, but the interests of human nature, of man in general, who belongs to no class, has no reality, who exists only in the misty realm of philosophical fantasy.

This German socialism, which took its schoolboy task so seriously and solemnly, and extolled its poor stock-in-trade in such a mountebank fashion, meanwhile gradually lost its pedantic innocence.

The fight of the Germans, and especially of the Prussian bourgeoisie, against feudal aristocracy and absolute monarchy, in other words, the liberal movement, became more earnest.

By this, the long-wished for opportunity was offered to "True" Socialism of confronting the political movement with the socialistic demands, of hurling the traditional anathemas against liberalism, against representative government, against bourgeois competition, bourgeois freedom of the press, bourgeois legislation, bourgeois liberty and equality, and of preaching to the masses that they had nothing to gain, and everything to lose, by this bourgeois movement. German socialism forgot, in the nick of time, that the French criticism, whose silly echo it was, presupposed the existence of modern bourgeois society, with its corresponding economic conditions of existence, and the political constitution adapted thereto, the very things whose attainment was the object of the pending struggle in Germany.

To the absolute governments, with their following of parsons, professors, country squires, and officials, it served as a welcome scarecrow against the threatening bourgeoisie.

It was a sweet finish, after the bitter pills of flogging and bullets, with which these same governments, just at that time, dosed the German working-class risings.

While this "True" Socialism thus served the government as a weapon for fighting the German bourgeoisie, it, at the same time, directly represented a reactionary interest, the interest of German philistines. In Germany, the petty-bourgeois class, a relic of the sixteenth century, and since then constantly cropping up again under the various forms, is the real social basis of the existing state of things.

To preserve this class is to preserve the existing state of things in Germany. The industrial and political supremacy of the bourgeoisie threatens it with certain destruction—on the one hand, from the concentration of capital; on the other, from the rise of a revolutionary proletariat. "True" Socialism appeared to kill these two birds with one stone. It spread like an epidemic.

The robe of speculative cobwebs, embroidered with flowers of rhetoric, steeped in the dew of sickly sentiment, this transcendental robe in which the German Socialists wrapped their sorry "eternal truths," all skin and bone, served to wonderfully increase the sale of their goods amongst such a public. And on its part German socialism recognized, more and more, its own calling as the bombastic representative of the petty-bourgeois philistine.

It proclaimed the German nation to be the model nation, and the German petty philistine to be the typical man. To every villainous meanness of this model man, it gave a hidden, higher, socialistic interpretation, the exact contrary of its real character. It went to the extreme length

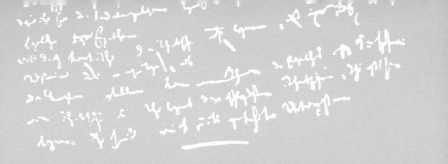

of directly opposing the "brutally destructive" tendency of communism, and of proclaiming its supreme and impartial contempt of all class struggles. With very few exceptions, all the so-called socialist and communist publications that now (1847) circulate in Germany belong to the domain of this foul and enervating literature.[7]

2. Conservative or Bourgeois Socialism

A part of the bourgeoisie is desirous of redressing social grievances in order to secure the continued existence of bourgeois society.

To this section belong economists, philanthropists, humanitarians, improvers of the condition of the working class, organizers of charity, members of societies for the prevention of cruelty to animals, temperance fanatics, hole-and-corner reformers of every imaginable kind. This form of socialism has, moreover, been worked out into complete systems.

We may cite Proudhon's *Philosophy of Poverty* as an example of this form.

The socialistic bourgeois want all the advantages of modern social conditions without the struggles and dangers necessarily resulting therefrom. They desire the existing state of society, minus its revolutionary and disintegrating elements. They wish for a bourgeoisie without a proletariat. The bourgeoisie naturally conceives the world in which it is supreme to be the best; and bourgeois socialism develops this comfortable conception into various more or less complete systems. In requiring the proletariat to carry out such a system, and thereby to march straightaway into the social New Jerusalem, it but requires in reality that the proletariat should remain within the bounds of existing society, but should cast away all its hateful ideas concerning the bourgeoisie.

A second, and more practical, but less systematic, form of this socialism sought to depreciate every revolutionary movement in the eyes of the working class by showing that no mere political reform, but only a change in the material conditions of existence, in economical relations, could be of any advantage to them. By changes in the material conditions of existence, this form of socialism, however, by no means understands abolition of the bourgeois relations of production, an abolition that can be affected only by a revolution, but administrative reforms, based on the continued existence of these relations; reforms, therefore, that in no respect affect the relations between capital and labor, but, at the best, lessen the cost, and simplify the administrative work of bourgeois government.

Bourgeois socialism attains adequate expression when, and only when, it becomes a mere figure of speech.

Free trade: for the benefit of the working class. Protective duties: for the benefit of the working class. Prison reform: for the benefit of the working class. This is the last word and the only seriously meant word of bourgeois socialism.

It is summed up in the phrase: the bourgeois is a bourgeois—for the benefit of the working class.

3. Critical-Utopian Socialism and Communism

We do not here refer to that literature which, in every great modern revolution, has always given voice to the demands of the proletariat, such as the writings of Babeuf and others.

The first direct attempts of the proletariat to attain its own ends, made in times of universal excitement when feudal society was being overthrown, necessarily failed, owing to the then undeveloped state of the proletariat, as well as to the absence of the economic conditions for its emancipation, conditions that had yet to be produced, and could be produced by the impending bourgeois epoch alone. The revolutionary literature that accompanied these first movements of the proletariat had necessarily a reactionary character. It inculcated universal asceticism and social leveling in its crudest form.

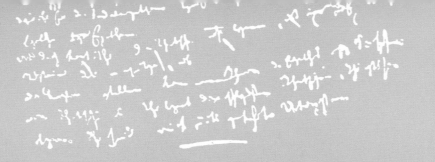

The socialist and communist systems, properly so called, those of Saint-Simon, Fourier, Owen, and others, spring into existence in the early undeveloped period, described above, of the struggle between proletariat and bourgeoisie (see Section 1. Bourgeois and Proletarians).

The founders of these systems see, indeed, the class antagonisms, as well as the action of the decomposing elements in the prevailing form of society. But the proletariat, as yet in its infancy, offers to them the spectacle of a class without any historical initiative or any independent political movement.

Since the development of class antagonism keeps even pace with the development of industry, the economic situation, as they find it, does not as yet offer to them the material conditions for the emancipation of the proletariat. They therefore search after a new social science, after new social laws, that are to create these conditions.

Historical action is to yield to their personal inventive action; historically created conditions of emancipation to fantastic ones; and the gradual, spontaneous class organization of the proletariat to an organization of society especially contrived by these inventors. Future history resolves itself, in their eyes, into the propaganda and the practical carrying out of their social plans.

In the formation of their plans, they are conscious of caring chiefly for the interests of the working class, as being the most suffering class. Only from the point of view of being the most suffering class does the proletariat exist for them.

The undeveloped state of the class struggle, as well as their own surroundings, causes Socialists of this kind to consider themselves far superior to all class antagonisms. They want to improve the condition of every member of society, even that of the most favored. Hence, they habitually appeal to society at large, without the distinction of class; nay, by preference, to the ruling class. For how can people when once they understand their system, fail to see in it the best possible plan of the best possible state of society?

Hence, they reject all political, and especially all revolutionary action; they wish to attain their ends by peaceful means, necessarily doomed to failure, and by the force of example, to pave the way for the new social gospel.

Such fantastic pictures of future society, painted at a time when the proletariat is still in a very undeveloped state and has but a fantastic conception of its own position, correspond with the first instinctive yearnings of that class for a general reconstruction of society.

But these socialist and communist publications contain also a critical element. They attack every principle of existing society. Hence, they are full of the most valuable materials for the enlightenment of the working class. The practical measures proposed in them—such as the abolition of the distinction between town and country, of the family, of the carrying on of industries for the account of private individuals, and of the wage system, the proclamation of social harmony, the conversion of the function of the state into a more superintendence of production—all these proposals point solely to the disappearance of class antagonisms which were, at that time, only just cropping up, and which, in these publications, are recognized in their earliest indistinct and undefined forms only. These proposals, therefore, are of a purely utopian character.

The significance of critical-utopian socialism and communism bears an inverse relation to historical development. In proportion as the modern class struggle develops and takes definite shape, this fantastic standing apart from the contest, these fantastic attacks on it, lose all practical value and all theoretical justifications. Therefore, although the originators of these systems were, in many respects, revolutionary, their disciples have, in every case, formed mere reactionary sects. They hold fast by the original views of their masters, in opposition to the progressive historical development of the proletariat. They, therefore, endeavor, and that consistently, to deaden the class struggle and to reconcile the class antagonisms. They still dream of experimental realization of their social utopias, of founding isolated phalanstères, of establishing "Home Colonies," or setting up a "Little Icaria"[8]—

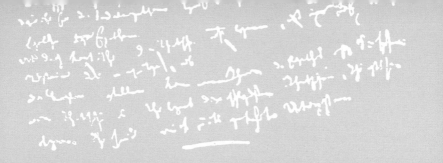

pocket editions of the New Jerusalem—and to realize all these castles in the air, they are compelled to appeal to the feelings and purses of the bourgeois. By degrees, they sink into the category of the reactionary conservative socialists depicted above, differing from these only by more systematic pedantry, and by their fanatical and superstitious belief in the miraculous effects of their social science.

They, therefore, violently oppose all political action on the part of the working class; such action, according to them, can only result from blind unbelief in the new gospel.

The Owenites in England, and the Fourierists in France, respectively, oppose the Chartists and the Réformistes.

Position of the Communists in Relation to the Various Existing Opposition Parties

Section II has made clear the relations of the Communists to the existing working-class parties, such as the Chartists in England and the Agrarian Reformers in America.

The Communists fight for the attainment of the immediate aims, for the enforcement of the momentary interests of the working class; but in the movement of the present, they also represent and take care of the future of that movement. In France, the Communists ally with the Social Democrats[9] against the conservative and radical bourgeoisie, reserving, however, the right to take up a critical position in regard to phases and illusions traditionally handed down from the great Revolution.

In Switzerland, they support the Radicals, without losing sight of the fact that this party consists of antagonistic elements, partly of Democratic Socialists, in the French sense, partly of radical bourgeois.

In Poland, they support the party that insists on an agrarian revolution as the prime condition for national emancipation, that party which fomented the insurrection of Krakow in 1846.

In Germany, they fight with the bourgeoisie whenever it acts in a revolutionary way, against the absolute monarchy, the feudal squirearchy, and the petty-bourgeoisie.

But they never cease, for a single instant, to instill into the working class the clearest possible recognition of the hostile antagonism between bourgeoisie and proletariat, in order that the German workers may straightway use, as so many weapons against the bourgeoisie, the social and political conditions that the bourgeoisie must necessarily introduce along with its supremacy, and in order that, after the fall of the reactionary classes in Germany, the fight against the bourgeoisie itself may immediately begin.

The Communists turn their attention chiefly to Germany, because that country is on the eve of a bourgeois revolution that is bound to be carried out under more advanced conditions of European civilization and with a much more developed proletariat than that of England was in the seventeenth, and France in the eighteenth century, and because the bourgeois revolution in Germany will be but the prelude to an immediately following proletarian revolution.

In short, the Communists everywhere support every revolutionary movement against the existing social and political order of things.

In all these movements, they bring to the front, as the leading question in each, the property question, no matter what its degree of development at the time.

Finally, they labor everywhere for the union and agreement of the democratic parties of all countries.

The Communists disdain to conceal their views and aims. They openly declare that their ends can be attained only by the forcible overthrow of all existing social conditions. Let the ruling classes tremble at a communist revolution. The proletarians have nothing to lose but their chains. They have a world to win.

WORKERS OF ALL COUNTRIES, UNITE!

Notes to the 1888 English edition and to the 1888 and 1890 German editions

[1] By bourgeoisie is meant the class of modern capitalists, owners of the means of social production and employers of wage labor. By proletariat, the class of modern wage laborers who, having no means of production of their own, are reduced to selling their labor power in order to live. [Engels, 1888 English edition]

[2] That is, all written history. In 1847, the pre-history of society, the social organization existing previous to recorded history, all but unknown. Since then, August von Haxthausen (1792–1866) discovered common ownership of land in Russia, Georg Ludwig von Maurer proved it to be the social foundation from which all Teutonic races started in history, and, by and by, village communities were found to be, or to have been, the primitive form of society everywhere from India to Ireland. The inner organization of this primitive communistic society was laid bare, in its typical form, by Lewis

Henry Morgan's (1818–61) crowning discovery of the true nature of the gens and its relation to the tribe. With the dissolution of the primeval communities, society begins to be differentiated into separate and finally antagonistic classes. I have attempted to retrace this dissolution in *Der Ursprung der Familie, des Privateigenthumus und des Staats*, second edition, Stuttgart, 1886. [Engels, 1888 English edition]

3 Guild-master, that is, a full member of a guild, a master within, not a head of a guild. [Engels, 1888 English edition]

4 This was the name given their urban communities by the townsmen of Italy and France, after they had purchased or conquered their initial rights of self-government from their feudal lords. [Engels, 1890 German edition]

"Commune" was the name taken in France by the nascent towns even before they had conquered from their feudal lords and masters local self-government and political rights as the "Third Estate." Generally speaking, for the economical development of the bourgeoisie, England is here taken as the typical country, for its political development, France. [Engels, 1888 English edition]

5 Not the English Restoration (1660–89), but the French Restoration (1814–30). [Engels, 1888 German edition]

6 This applies chiefly to Germany, where the landed aristocracy and squirearchy have large portions of their estates cultivated for their own account by stewards, and are, moreover, extensive beetroot-sugar manufacturers and distillers of potato spirits. The wealthier British aristocracy are, as yet, rather above that; but they, too, know how to make up for declining rents by lending their names to floaters or more or less shady joint-stock companies. [Engels, 1888 German edition]

7 The revolutionary storm of 1848 swept away this whole shabby tendency and cured its protagonists of the desire to dabble in socialism. The chief representative and classical type of this tendency is Mr. Karl Gruen. [Engels, 1888 German edition]

8 *Phalanstères* were socialist colonies on the plan of Charles Fourier; Icaria was the name given by Cabet to his Utopia and, later on, to his American Communist colony. [Engels, 1888 English edition]

"Home Colonies" were what Owen called his communist model societies. *Phalanstères* was the name of the public palaces planned by Fourier. Icaria was the name given to the Utopian land of fancy, whose communist institutions Cabet portrayed. [Engels, 1890 German edition]

9 The party then represented in Parliament by Ledru-Rollin, in literature by Louis Blanc, in the daily press by the Reforme. The name of Social-Democracy signifies, with these its inventors, a section of the Democratic or Republican Party more or less tinged with socialism. [Engels, 1888 English edition]

THE COMMUNIST MANIFESTO
IMMEDIATE IMPACT

"Our age, the age of democracy, is breaking," Engels wrote with barely contained excitement at the news of the first French revolt in 1848, just as he and Marx had handed over the text to the printers. All that the *Communist Manifesto* had predicted looked like it was coming to pass. Yet the book itself could not take any credit. Rebellion had broken out before the ink was dry on the page and the initial print run was for just 1,000 copies—in German.

The original version was published on or about February 24, 1848. It had been typeset by the Workers' Educational Association in London and rushed to a printer near Liverpool Street. Its first readers were German émigrés—the document was serialized in the *Deutsche Londoner Zeitung*, a liberal weekly for German refugees in London—together with a handful of French, Belgians, and a few members of the Chartist Movement in London.

The main circulation in the next few months was among members of the Communist League in London and Brussels. The *Manifesto*'s whole tone and outlook were deliberately set in international terms, but to most of its early readers it must have appeared essentially related to conflicts between the communism defined by Marx and Engels and the socialist beliefs of other groups.

Despite the excitement felt by the Communist League at the *Manifesto*'s arrival, the publication date must have meant that it did nothing to precipitate, and had no influence upon, the February Revolution in Paris, which broke out within a few days. Nor can it have had any effect on the

German risings of that year. The *Manifesto* does not appear to have been known in Germany until at least May, and perhaps even June, of 1848. Riots first broke out in Berlin on March 15.

If anything, Marx and Engels's most popular work looked in danger of being instantly out of date. The "holy alliance" singled out for special mention in the book's opening paragraph already comprised names of the past. French prime minister François Guizot was dismissed on February 23, King Louis-Philippe abdicated the next day—after the National Guard refused to cheer for him—and the Austrian chancellor, Metternich, was gone within three weeks.

Some copies of the *Manifesto* did arrive in Paris by March, and so did Marx and his family. He had been expelled from Belgium for the "revolting scurrility and savagery" of his attacks on the Belgian government in articles written for the *Deutsche-Brusseler-Zeitung*—those who were expelling him had not even seen the first copies of the *Manifesto*. Marx was preparing to leave the country anyway. He and his comrades were dashing off to where the action was.

Schapper, Bauer, and Moll joined Marx and Engels in the French capital and the Communist League's headquarters was hastily relocated to Paris—under the guise of the German Workers' Club. They passed a proposal to wear blood-red ribbons on their jackets and got straight down to business: planning revolution.

Top: the barricades in the rue St Martin in Paris, made of overturned wooden carts: the unmistakable symbol of revolutionary uprisings in Paris, copied in most of the capital cities of Europe in 1848.

Above: the Paris Commune of 1848 that followed the revolution.

The revolution that began in Paris in February 1848 had spread to Germany within weeks. Here, the citizens of Altenburg erect barricades to force their duke to accept a liberal constitution.

Marx and Engels were convinced that Germany would be the next country to revolt. And what they needed was an immediate diet of propaganda in the form of a revised version of the *Manifesto*. The fact that Germany had no proletariat to rise up meant that this would be a bourgeois revolution. The *Manifesto*'s demands therefore had to be watered down, to be made more palatable to the German middle classes.

And so it was that the *Demands of the Communist Party in Germany* contained only four of the ten points in the original *Manifesto*, including setting up a national bank and progressive income tax, measures sure to appeal to bourgeois interests. The demands appeared in papers in Berlin, Düsseldorf, and Marx's hometown of Trier.

The next item on the agenda was raising the consciousness of the elusive German worker. The members of the Communist League set about this task at once, leaving Paris by the end of March to spread the word in their home towns in Germany. As one comrade wrote, "The League has dissolved; it is everywhere and nowhere."

Marx went to Cologne for a second time, to start a radical newspaper to encourage the revolutionary atmosphere witnessed in France. The *Neue Rheinische Zeitung* was set up with what remained of an inheritance from his mother. Its editorial board contained former members of the Communist League, such as Wilhelm Wolff, but it was effectively—in the words of Engels—"a simple dictatorship by Marx."

The next 12 months in Germany were described by Marx as "the mad year." He appears to have been in a towering rage for most of the time as the progress of revolution ebbed and flowed. He was also becoming aware of the dilemma at the heart of the *Manifesto*. The book argued that communists should encourage the proletariat to support the bourgeoisie "whenever it acts in a revolutionary way"; at the same time it emphasized the natural antagonism that exists between the two of them. It was a confusing message.

In any event, neither the *Manifesto* nor the articles in the *Neue Rheinische Zeitung* could help the rebellion in Germany. The infant parliaments in Germany and Prussia— set up after the riots in March—fell apart by September and the counter-revolution began. After numerous court appearances (during which Marx often argued his case so brilliantly that the jury found him not guilty), the Prussian authorities finally ordered his deportation and that of most of his staff. The paper's last issue was printed in red ink with the parting words: "emancipation of the working class!"

An uprising of the proletariat in the heart of capitalism—England—had been conspicuous by its absence during 1848, the year of revolutions. Marx wrote at the start of 1849, "England, the country that turns whole nations into its proletarians ... England seems to be the rock against which the revolutionary waves break, the country where the new society is stifled in the womb."

The first English edition of the *Communist Manifesto* did not appear until 1850. Not that the original English translation would have done much to inspire the English working classes to follow their continental cousins into revolt. The famous opening line of the *Manifesto* first appeared as "A frightful hobgoblin is stalking the land"— more Brothers Grimm than blueprint for rebellion. Helen Macfarlane's original translation was not superseded by Samuel Moore's more famous version—"A specter is haunting Europe"—until 1888, and by then Marx had been dead for five years.

1848: Year of Revolutions

The year of 1848–49 represented "the mad year" not just for Marx, but for the whole of Western Europe. It was ironic that the world's most famous revolutionary manifesto should be published that very year, yet have so little influence on it. By coincidence, a wave of revolution was sweeping through France, Germany, and the Austrian Empire, much of it surging forth without direction or control. There was a strong element of spontaneity to many of the uprisings.

What had brought both the proletariat and the middle classes onto the streets? As had been evident in the French Revolution, they seemed to be calling for different things. The workers wanted bread and jobs, whereas the bourgeoisie wanted power in the form of the vote.

Poor harvests in 1846 and 1847, and a blight that turned potatoes black—causing the notorious famine in Ireland—had led to rising food prices. Discontent among the urban poor was further fueled by an industrial downturn:

By the spring the revolution had spread to Vienna, the heart of the Habsburg empire, and soon all the monsters—including the Austrian foreign minister, Metternich—named in the first paragraphs of the *Manifesto* had resigned.

the great capitalist machine appeared to be faltering and unemployment was rising. Not only was food more expensive, but the work to pay for it was harder to find.

"Can you not hear them [the working classes] repeating incessantly that all who are above them are incapable and unworthy of governing them?" asked the French philosopher Alexis de Tocqueville in 1847. The governments of the day appeared both unwilling and unable to respond to the changing economic and social conditions. The middle classes wanted extended suffrage and more accountable government, and they were also prepared to resort to street fighting to get their demands met, often using students in the front line.

The first country to teeter on the edge was the revolution's natural home: France. It was the bourgeoisie who led the February riots that broke out in Paris, but they were fighting alongside the working class. The proletariat's call for the "right to work" was appeased with the creation of National Workshops, a "job creation" scheme for the unemployed on public works projects. The government's abolition of these workshops less than four months later was the signal for the urban poor to raise the red flags on the barricades.

All the revolutions inspired by the February uprising in Paris followed the same pattern. Excited crowds would gather to hear news of the revolution in France. The government, fearing trouble, would send in the army, and minor skirmishes would erupt between the people and the police. This was the scene in the Rhineland (March 3), Vienna

(March 12), Berlin (March 15), and Milan (March 18), with most of the revolutions taking place in one city of each nation. Between February and June of that year Paris, Vienna, Berlin, Prague, Budapest, Rome, and Milan witnessed revolts that toppled governments or frightened them into introducing hastily contrived reform.

The tenuous alliance between the bourgeoisie and the proletariat fell apart in the second revolution in France that year—known as the "Bloody June Days." This time around, the uprising was ruthlessly suppressed by republican troops. More than 1,000 people were killed in three days, and thousands more were sent to prison or into exile. The provisional government then created the Constitution of the Second Republic and gave France the opportunity to vote for its president by universal manhood suffrage—the first country in Europe to achieve this goal. This move was guaranteed to appease the middle classes at least.

But when the French voted overwhelmingly for Louis-Napoleon (nephew of Napoleon Bonaparte), whose campaign shamelessly exploited his family connections by claiming that his name was his program, Marx saw this as evidence that democracy would never work. The message in the *Manifesto* seemed confirmed: the workers must be in control themselves for there to be any hope of an egalitarian society.

The year 1848 was the closest either Marx or Engels came to witnessing revolution firsthand—albeit a fledgling one and short-lived. The rest of their lives (with the notable

Louis-Napoleon with his son Eugène, after declaring himself Emperor Napoleon III. His election after the revolution had deposed the French monarch, Louis-Philippe, convinced Marx that democracy would not work.

The French emperor Napoleon III (right, seated in a boat): the main winner of the revolution of 1848. His reign ended two decades later in the Franco-Prussian War and the Paris Commune of 1871.

exception of 1871) would be spent plotting and planning for a venture that would never be realized. But in that year they were in the thick of the action.

Within 12 months it was all over. Wherever the workers had raised their heads above the barricades they had been pitilessly suppressed. The army had returned an emperor to power in Austria, and uprisings in Vienna and Berlin had been brought under control. The King of Prussia had dissolved the Prussian assembly and formed a new government under the reactionary Count Brandenburg. Europe's monarchs had merely adjusted their crowns, but had not let them slip to the floor.

In France, Louis-Napoleon used a *coup d'état* to proclaim himself Napoleon III. And in London a massive demonstration by the Chartists—which frightened the government into appointing the elderly Duke of Wellington to command the defense of the city—ended peacefully. In Germany, any hopes that the *Manifesto* may have held out for a bourgeois revolution turned out to be merely a pipe dream. "The bourgeoisie did not raise a finger; they simply allowed the people to fight for them," complained Marx in the *Neue Rheinische Zeitung*. The proletariat was on its own.

There were other factors stacked up against the *Manifesto*'s dream scenario: the absence of any coordinated revolutionary leadership, and the fear of the bourgeoisie that things might go too far, also contributed to the outcome. As the English historian G. M. Trevelyan put it: "The year 1848 was the turning point at which European history did not turn."

Decline and Fall: The Collapse
of the Communist League

Tired of Marx's inflammatory rhetoric, the authorities closed down the *Neue Rheinische Zeitung*, and Marx and his family were expelled from Prussia. They returned to France, traveling on false passports. But any hope of keeping the revolution there alive through his journalism soon evaporated—all the revolutionary newspapers had been shut down in the wake of a royalist backlash. Government soldiers made short shrift of a mass demonstration on June 13, arresting the ringleaders and dispersing the demonstrators. Foreign troublemakers were next on the list. Marx was officially exiled to Morbihan, a region in the malaria-infested marshes of Brittany—he described the order as a "veiled attempt on his life." Having declared that he was leaving France, the next task was to find a country that would take him. Germany and Belgium did not want him back, and even Switzerland refused his passport application. So it was that Marx was forced to seek refuge in England. He arrived in Dover on the SS *City of Boulogne* on August 27, 1849, under the name "Charles Marx, profession Dr," to begin what he referred to as the "long, sleepless night of exile."

Meanwhile, the *Manifesto*'s coconspirator was putting the book's words into action. Engels had joined a military unit of revolutionary forces fighting in southwestern Germany to defend the provisional government. But after four defeats in as many weeks, he retreated to Switzerland to nurse his wounds. Marx wrote to the "General"—his

Jenny von Westfalen, Marx's long-suffering wife. The family was constantly in debt, and the poverty and squalor in which they were forced to live in London brought about the deaths of two of their children.

nickname for Engels—that he must join him at once: "In London we shall get down to business."

Marx and Engels were optimistic that there would be a fresh revolutionary outbreak in Europe. The new headquarters for the Communist League was quickly established at the London offices of the German Workers' Education Society, the scene of Marx and Engels's victory at the League's second congress back in November 1847. Despite its attempts to consolidate socialist factions throughout Europe, the League was still only one of many political groups of a revolutionary diaspora.

Marx was elected to the Committee to Aid German Refugees—one of the families most in need being his own. His wife, Jenny, gave birth to their fourth child shortly after arriving from France, but during the next two years both this child and another would die, as the family faced unhealthy living conditions and dire poverty in their Dean Street apartment. A report by a Prussian spy during this period confirmed that they had sold most of their possessions and that they did not own "one solid piece of furniture."

The League's Great Windmill Street offices did offer Marx some distraction from his distressing personal circumstances. He soon took control of business, and the intrigues and battles for supremacy that ensued were reminiscent of the old days in Paris and Brussels. A busy timetable of activities included discussions on communism during the first two days of the week, with a slightly lighter timetable toward the end, including singing, dancing, and drawing classes. Saturday evening was devoted to "music, recitations, and reading interesting newspaper articles."

Some of the most interesting articles of the time were to be found in Marx's new journal, the *Revue*. In one of them, Marx challenged the widely held verdict that the French Revolution of 1848 had failed. His alternative view was that success would have been a disaster, because it was only by a series of setbacks that a revolutionary party could hone its skills. "The revolution made progress, forged ahead, not by its immediate tragi-comic achievements, but on the contrary by the creation of a powerful, united counter-revolution. The revolution is dead!—*Long live the revolution!*"

Much of the *Revue* was given over to the petty in-fighting and attacks on other members of the tiny German refugee community that so often characterized Marx and Engels's time with the Communist League. This form of financial suicide—attacking the *Revue*'s only potential readership—soon scuppered the newspaper's chances and it went under after just five issues.

The success of the League depended on prospects for a "renewed upsurge of the revolution," but as 1850 unrolled, this was looking less and less likely. As Engels wrote in his *History of the Communist League*: "The industrial crisis of 1847, which had paved the way for the Revolution of 1848, had been overcome; a new, unprecedented period of industrial prosperity had set in; whoever had eyes to see and used them must have clearly realized that the revolutionary storm of 1848 was gradually spending itself."

A bloody handprint on a Russian communist poster. This was an early communist symbol, and a symptom of Marx and Engels's changing attitude to violence—recognizing that it would be a critical component of revolution.

In the end, the Communist League was to self-combust in dramatic fashion. A riotous meeting of the central committee on September 1, 1850, resulted in a violent disagreement between Marx and August Willich, one of the malcontents who wanted to see more signs of revolutionary action. Willich (Engels's military commander and a crack shot) challenged Marx to a duel, which he sensibly refused. The man who stood in for Marx, Conrad Schramm, had never fired a pistol before. News reached the comrades that Schramm had been killed, but as they reminisced sadly about him, he burst into the room with a bandaged head. A glancing bullet had merely knocked him unconscious, and by the time he awoke, Willich had left, thinking him dead.

Schramm may have escaped with his life, but the Communist League in London was definitely no more. At its final meeting on September 15, 1850, Marx proposed that the Central Committee should be transferred to Cologne because the London group appeared incapable of working together. Unhappily, the comrades in Cologne had problems of their own. All 11 committee members were in jail awaiting trial on conspiracy charges and, following the month-long "Cologne Communist Trial," seven members were imprisoned. The League was dead in the water, and many years were to pass before Marx or Engels joined any other organization.

In his last address to the Communist League, Marx claimed that during 1848–49 its members had proved themselves "in the press, on the barricades, and on the

A membership card for the International Working Men's Association, formed in London's Covent Garden in 1864, with Marx on the General Council. By the time of its first European congress, the "International" had more than 25,000 members.

battlefields." But perhaps more importantly for world history, the manifesto it had caused to be written transmitted a strong new message previously propagated only in secret. In Marx's words, that message was "now on everyone's lips and … preached openly in the market."

The International and the Paris Commune

Although Marx may have been optimistic about the *Manifesto*'s survival into posterity, Engels struck a more realistic tone when he later wrote that, at that precise point in history, the *Manifesto* seemed to be "doomed to oblivion."

Even Marx had to admit that, while England experienced a period of bourgeois prosperity, "there can be no talk of a real revolution … A new revolution is possible only in consequence of a new crisis." Armed with back issues of *The Economist*, he retreated to the British Museum's reading room to devote himself to the study of political economy in order to determine the cause and conditions of this hungrily expected crisis. Marx claimed that he had eagerly seized the opportunity to "withdraw from the public stage into the study" and work on Volume I of *Das Kapital,* which analyzed the capitalist process of production. As the author bitterly noted, "I don't suppose anyone has ever written about 'money' when so short of the stuff."

For ten years the socialist groups in Britain appeared to fall into a stupor, and it was not until 1860 that the proletariat began to rouse themselves from their long sleep.

As the historian Eric Hobsbawm has noted, this awakening was a "curious amalgam of political and industrial action ... which was most significantly 'international' on two fronts: it occurred simultaneously in various countries" and "it was inseparable from the international solidarity of the working classes."

On September 28, 1864 a meeting was called at St. Martin's Hall in Covent Garden to form the International Working Men's Association. Marx attended simply as an observer, but by the end of the evening he found himself elected onto the General Council. It was largely because of his hard work that the organization did not collapse within 12 months. The Council contained a huge diversity of people with widely differing aims who agreed on almost nothing.

Marx had to be dragged from his sickbed to rescue the International's new creed, *Address to the Working Class*, from sliding into banality and utopianism. The *Address* lacked the revolutionary predictions and enthusiastic rhetoric of the *Communist Manifesto*. As he confessed to Engels: "It will take time before the revival of the movement allows the old boldness of language to be used." Still, it did include a number of statistics from *Das Kapital* to back up his claim that the "misery of the working masses" was as evident in 1864 as it had been in 1848. And the *Address* finished with the familiar cry: "Proletarians of all countries, unite!"

The International did have some small successes in disrupting British industry, and boasted 25,173 members by the time of its first European congress in Geneva. But the

The surrender of Napoleon III to Prussian forces after the French defeat and his own capture at the Battle of Sedan. His capture launched a series of events leading to the first proletarian revolution anywhere in Europe.

organization's greatest moment came in 1871 when the people of Paris rose up against the national government that had led them to siege and starvation during the Franco-Prussian War. This was the famous Paris Commune—not exactly the result of the *Communist Manifesto*, but evidence for its authors that they were working along the right lines.

The war that precipitated the Paris Commune had begun in July the previous year. It started with the Prussian Chancellor Bismarck's successful attempt to goad the French emperor, followed shortly afterward by the complete collapse of the French army in a series of battles, including Sedan on September 2, 1870, where Napoleon III was captured along with 100,000 of his soldiers. Two days later, a bloodless revolution in Paris ended France's Second Empire and a new government of national defense was set up.

After a further crushing French defeat at Metz, when 180,000 more soldiers surrendered, the new French government hastily signed an armistice at Versailles in January 1871. But the citizens of Paris, who had held out against the Prussian siege of their city for six long months, were furious at this capitulation. And when the French government, worried about this show of defiance, tried to disarm the National Guard, the Parisians resisted, seizing control of their city. The government of the Third Republic fled to Versailles.

A new municipal government—the first government in history that could possibly claim to be proletarian—was elected on March 26, 1871. Half of its 81 members had been involved in the French Labor movement and most of them belonged to the International. None of them had any political experience, and the Commune as a whole lacked direction. This was particularly serious because it had to fight a war if it was to survive at all.

What the Commune did have were some "heaven-storming" revolutionary policies—as Marx called them in *Civil War in France*—including separating the church from the state and seizing all church property, banning religion from schools, postponing debt obligations, and abolishing interest on debts (the last two would have been particularly welcome in the Marx household, as would another measure to stop pawnshops from selling goods, such as the tools of skilled workers that had been pawned during the war).

Napoleon III meets the Prussian chancellor Otto von Bismarck. French and Prussian troops worked together to storm Paris and put an end to the 1871 Commune, with more than 30,000 Parisian "Communards" slaughtered in the process.

As someone with impeccable revolutionary credentials —Lenin—was to testify later, the Commune was "the first dress rehearsal in world history of the socialist revolution of the working class ... which, for the first time set up its power by its own might with the purpose of setting the whole of society free from the system of enslavement and securing its own political and social emancipation."

The whole business lasted for just 72 days—albeit, in Lenin's words, "epoch-making" ones. Large crowds were listening to a concert in the Tuileries gardens on the day that the Versailles forces, supported by the Prussian army, broke through the city's defenses. The army gunned down up to 30,000 Communards, many of them unarmed, losing only 900 of their own forces in the battles at the barricades.

Gun carriages defending the fledgling Paris Commune in 1871. The Communards were eventually overwhelmed by a combined attack from French and Prussian troops. By the time Marx wrote his address to the people of Paris, the revolution was over.

Far more died during that last week in May 1871—known as *la semaine sanglante* ("the bloody week")—than in any of the battles of the Franco-Prussian War. As many as 50,000 more were arrested, some of them deported to the French penal colony of New Caledonia in the Pacific. Many died in prison. Those who escaped went into exile in Switzerland, Belgium, England, or farther afield. By the time Marx delivered his 50-page address to the people of Paris—later published as *The Civil War in France*—on behalf of the International, it was an epitaph.

The Paris Commune was the closest the authors of the *Manifesto* would ever get to seeing its principles put into practice during their lifetime. Yet much of the social legislation passed by the Commune was reformist rather than revolutionary. Trade unions and workers' cooperatives were allowed to restart vacant factories, but a suggestion to take over all factories was rejected. Not even the Paris Commune was ready to take the *Manifesto* at its word.

The Emergence of Marxism

In 1879, eight years after the bloody events in Paris, Queen Victoria's eldest daughter—the wife of the future German emperor Friedrich Wilhelm—asked the Liberal politician and future colonial secretary Sir Mountstuart Grant Duff to find out about Marx for her. He duly invited Marx to a three-hour lunch at the Devonshire Club and afterward wrote a glowing testimonial: "Altogether my impression of Marx, allowing for his being at the opposite pole of opinion from oneself, was

not at all unfavourable and I would gladly meet him again." And he added: "It will not be he who, whether he wishes it or not, will turn the world upside down." The coauthor of the *Manifesto* was now in the final decade of his life, and Grant Duff's assessment seemed a likely one. When Marx died in 1883, the *London Daily News* reported: "He had lived to see the portions of his theories which once terrified Emperors and Chancellors die out ... English working men would not care to be identified with these principles."

By the end of the century, capitalism was clearly more successful in Europe's industrialized nations than Marx had predicted; the middle classes were growing rather than shrinking; and living standards were rising. Anyone might have been forgiven for writing off Marx before there was ever such a thing as Marxism.

Marx's final years were deeply disappointing to him. The immediate consequences of the defeat of the Commune were disastrous for the French Labor Movement, as a period of severe repression followed. Paris remained under martial law for five years, and the International was practically forced out of existence. Armed with new political powers, the police rounded up political activists, who were given heavy sentences. The leading activists of the French working class were now dead, imprisoned, or in exile.

This marked the start of the slow decline of Marx's energies. The last congress of the International had been in 1869. After the Commune's collapse, Marx called for a full congress in The Hague, where, with so many communists in

The illustrated banner of the Dockers' Union in London immediately before the Great Dock Strike of 1889. It was eventually resolved after the intervention of the Roman Catholic Archbishop of Westminster, but was the most bitter strike in England of the century.

town, shopkeepers barred their doors and a local paper advised women and children not to venture outdoors. Here, Marx forced through a motion that removed the headquarters of the International to New York. The move was a deliberate death sentence for the organization; a way of suppressing the internal struggles between Marxists and followers of his antagonists, Pierre Proudhon and Mikhail Bakunin. Marx's most famous long-running argument was with the influential anarchist Bakunin, who had arrived in London in 1861 after a period in prison in Russia and tried to hijack the leadership of the International. Posterity credits Bakunin with predicting the authoritarian flaws at the heart of Marxism.

Marx was coming to believe the struggle was going to take a long time: "You will have to pass through 15, 20, perhaps 50 years, of civil and international wars," he commented, "not merely in order to change conditions, but to change yourselves, and make yourselves fit to take over political power."

And yet, paradoxically, the ideas of the *Communist Manifesto* were finally taking root among a new generation of radicals who accepted the analysis of Marx and Engels. Both men had matured in their thinking—not so much that they could resist rushing out a new German edition during the Paris Commune, but enough for them to write long prefaces to the new editions to put the words into a fresh context. Marx's preface to the Russian edition of 1882—importantly predicting a possible revolution in Russia—was the last published writing he ever did.

The Great Street-Railway Strike in New York City. Often it was Marx's great rivals, the anarchists, who were using their strategy of the strike weapon with the most effectiveness.

By then the German social democrats had won 12 seats in the Reichstag—"never has a proletariat conducted itself so magnificently," wrote Engels—and they had supported the call of their Belgian colleagues to convene a second international socialist congress that same year of 1881. The comrades met in the tiny Swiss town of Chur and the result was the second Socialist International, with contested elections and proper representatives.

But the arguments continued, as the followers of Bakunin—the anarchists—urged their alternative strategy: using the strike weapon. In the 1880s it was anarchists who were organizing the campaign in the United States for an eight-hour day, involving demonstrations of more than 100,000 workers. In 1886, eight of them were sentenced to death in Chicago.

These internal battles dominated the first four international congresses of the Second International, and in 1896 the anarchists were prevented from speaking by the German social democrat leader Wilhelm Liebknecht and Marx's daughter Eleanor Aveling. Yet such was the ideological confusion that, in the end, it was the German social democrats who finally split from the Marxist "Spartacists" over their attitude to World War I.

Editions of the *Manifesto* were still churning forth. "At present, it is doubtless the most widely circulated, the most international product of all socialist literature, the common programme of many millions of workers of all countries from Siberia to California," wrote Engels.

THE MANIFESTO'S LEGACY

Marx died stateless and without a legal will in 1883, and was buried in Highgate Cemetery in London, where his grave remains a site of pilgrimage for Marxists from around the world. His enormous collection of letters and notebooks was handed over to Engels to enable him to complete Marx's life's work. And for more than a decade Engels struggled to finish *Das Kapital* before dying of cancer in 1895, his ashes scattered off Beachy Head in Sussex. The third and final volume of *Das Kapital* was not published until 1894, in Germany. A pirated English translation came out in New York and was a runaway best-seller because of a mis-understanding in Wall Street about its subject matter.

For most of their lives, the hope that their predictions would come true—with what the *Manifesto* calls "the forcible overthrow of all existing social conditions"—seemed remote. But it was only 23 years after Engels's death that the ideas he and Marx had introduced to the world were put into practice. This was the moment in history when a handful of youthful idealists—two generations on from those who had first read the *Manifesto*'s call to arms—suddenly transformed themselves into national leaders and turned their communist creed into something Marx would probably not have recognized.

In 1900 in Russia, a young revolutionary was released from prison in Siberia. His crime had been to agitate against the Tsarist regime of the time. Vladimir Ilyich Lenin—his real surname was Ulyanov—lost no time in establishing himself at the heart of Russia's Marxist party. An ardent

Karl Marx's tomb in Highgate cemetery in London, where he was buried in 1883. Since then it has become a place of pilgrimage for Marxists from all over the world. By coincidence, the motif of gigantic busts and statues—larger than lifesize—has appealed to Marxists ever since.

follower of Marx, Lenin believed that the longed-for revolution would take place in Russia.

Apart from Marx's writings, what really influenced Lenin was the fate of the Paris Commune. "The Commune lost because it compromised and recoiled," he wrote, and he was determined that—should he successfully lead an uprising in Russia—there would be no compromise with his enemies, and no quarter given them to enable them to counterattack.

Lenin and his party were indeed to forge a revolution in Russia, in 1917. It was the first successful revolution in the name of Marx. But it emerged, not from the proletarian masses as Marx and Engels had predicted, but from a small group of revolutionaries and intellectuals who stepped into the power vacuum created by the abdication of Tsar Nicholas II. And far from putting the ideals of the *Communist Manifesto* into practice, Lenin required such ruthlessness to fight for his revolution through civil war and economic crisis that he became a different kind of tsar. He transformed himself into an instrument of absolute power, realizing only when it was too late how that power might be abused in the wrong hands.

The immediate aftermath of the Russian Revolution was a heady period, when soldiers were given the right to elect their officers, men and women were treated equally, and workers' committees were given power over business. Land was put into public ownership, and the different nations of what became the Soviet Union were briefly given the right to decide their own futures. It was a time of striking creativity, and thrilling freedom in art, design, and poetry—

Top: **Lenin speaking in Red Square, Moscow, on the first anniversary of the Russian Revolution, in October 1918. This is the classic picture of the world's first successful revolutionary.**

Above: **a Russian civil war poster from 1920 asks, "Have you enlisted?"**

Lenin presides over an early meeting of the Bolshevik Council of People's Commissars, or Sovnarkom, at which Trotsky was also present. Lenin's years in power saw a disastrous increase in central control over the workings of party and nation.

often under the influence of the Modern Movement, using arresting images of industrialization in every medium.

This was one of the stranger results of the *Communist Manifesto*, as the artists of the new regime tried to develop a "pure proletarian" culture. There was the bizarre Symphony of Labor, performed in 1922 by workers and soldiers from Baku, with instruments including aircraft engines, cannons, and factory sirens. Then there was the poet Andrei Gastev, author of "Factory Whistles, Rails, and Tower," who urged the "the idea of subordinating people to mechanisms and the mechanization of man"—and the new regime approved so much that they made him director of the Central Institute of Labor.

But this was also a period of rising violence in the countryside as famine took hold, and even worse violence once the country descended into civil war. And on April 30, 1918, after a failed assassination attempt against Lenin, 500 people in Petrograd were shot in reprisal. "We stand for organized terror," said secret police chief Felix Dzerzhinsky. "Terror is an absolute necessity in time of revolution."

To the astonishment of his followers, Lenin abandoned many of the original communist principles laid down in the *Manifesto* soon after he and his party were securely in power. In the spring of 1921, he imposed the New Economic Policy in an effort to counter the combined effects of World War I, civil war, and the overly ambitious attempt to reshape the economy along communist lines in a matter of months, rather than years. Private enterprise was

Lenin (left) and Stalin in 1922, two years before Lenin's death. He came to distrust Stalin's brutal methods, but acted too late to prevent his rise to power, with disastrous consequences.

encouraged, trade unions were denied a say in management, and trade with capitalist countries was encouraged. The United States was allowed to provide starvation relief to ten million Russians.

To avoid opposition, Lenin began the first of what would be a terrible history of "purges," throwing 136,000 members out of the party. It was the face of things to come. When a stroke paralyzed the right side of his body in December 1922, Lenin realized too late what the instrument of power he had created might mean in somebody else's hands. When he died in January 1924, one of the greatest specters of the twentieth century, Josef Stalin, was waiting in the wings.

The truth about the system that emerged in the Soviet Union is not controversial—under Lenin's successor, it became possibly the most tyrannical regime in a century of tyrannical regimes, and certainly a close rival to Nazi Germany. But it is still an uncomfortable truth, because so many enthusiasts, inspired by the ideals of the *Communist Manifesto* in Western Europe, were duped into believing otherwise. Between the great wars of the twentieth century—the intellectual high tide of the *Manifesto*—many left-of-center admirers made the journey to Moscow and wrote long paeans of praise to the new system.

Socialists the world over looked at the first of Stalin's five-year plans—the first set a target rise in industrial output by 235.9 percent from 1928—with pride and admiration. And it is true that the Soviet dash to

industrialization and the rapid progress in education was impressive. Yet all the time, hidden behind the propaganda, the purges and murders were accelerating, and the terrible starvation of peasants after farm collectivization was taking unthinkable numbers: millions in the Ukraine alone.

Having positioned himself to control the new Soviet Union after Lenin's death, Stalin unveiled a policy that was described as "socialism in one country." It was an important shift away from the internationalism of the *Communist Manifesto*, which famously decreed that "workingmen have no country." Men like Leon Trotsky and his allies had believed that Russia's revolution was doomed unless it spread to other countries in Western Europe. Stalin realized this was a hopeless dream, at least immediately. His communism was tinged with a heavy helping of nationalism—precisely the opposite of what Marx and Engels had preached. But then patriotism seemed to give him an excuse for the terrible ordeal he was to inflict on his own country.

By 1929 Stalin had also won the debate against his coleader Nikolai Bukharin over the kind of new-style capitalism among the peasants that Lenin had produced, permitting small farms and private ownership. Stalin's policy was to drive the peasants off the land and into the factories, and to destroy the power of the richer peasants—the so-called kulaks—by forcing the pattern of small farms across Russia into a new system of state collectives.

The campaign was one of the great disasters of the century. Up to five million kulaks were deported to Siberia,

Generations after Lenin's death, Russians still revered his memory enough to queue in freezing conditions to visit his tomb in Red Square. The tomb remains there, an embarrassment for Russia's twenty-first-century leaders.

Far left: **Lenin's successors—Stalin, Rvkov, Kamenev, and Zinoviev—in 1925; within a few years, only Stalin remained.**

Left: **Leningrad factory workers listen to a report of the trial and execution of Zinoviev, Kamenev, and 14 others on false charges of plotting against Stalin and murdering Kirov.**

killing 1.5 million of them in the first few months alone, as the army drove them off the land. The peasants fought back, slaughtering more than half the cattle in Russia; however, within five years 70 percent of them had been forced to join collective farms—but not before millions had died in the resulting famines.

The city of Moscow doubled in size in just over a decade as the peasants transformed themselves into factory workers—although there was little freedom here, either. Under Stalin's rule, strikes were redefined as "sabotage," and after 1939, employees were fired if they were once more than 20 minutes late for work.

Meanwhile a new élite known as the *nomenklatura* began to emerge under Stalin's guidance. This was the cadre of administrators who ruled—in theory on behalf of the proletariat, but in practice the agents of a tyrannical regime that answered only to itself. It ruled by fear, but was itself ruled by fear.

After the assassination of Sergei Kirov in 1934—the only man likely to replace Stalin—the terrible purges began inside the party. Stalin's new People's Commissariat for Internal Affairs (or NKVD) rounded up tens of thousands of party members at night; many were never seen again. Stalin's former rivals were put on public trial and shot. Neighbors were encouraged to denounce neighbors; rumor, innuendo, and administrative oversight condemned millions to a fate in a world worthy of Franz Kafka. According to one of many widely differing estimates, up to 3.5 million people

Stalin at the height of his power, the successful war leader in 1946. His brutality was ignored for decades by admirers in Western Europe, but after his death the truth about his murderous purges was revealed by his successor.

were sent to the Gulag labor camps in Siberia, and more than half of those died of cold and hunger. An estimated 1.5 million more were executed outright. In 1937, Stalin turned his attention to the army. As many as 35,000 officers were purged—on the very eve of war, as it turned out—with most being either arrested or executed. "We will destroy any such enemy, be he Bolshevik or not, we will destroy his kin, his family," said Stalin in a toast to the October Revolution. "Anyone who by his actions and thoughts—yes, his thoughts—encroaches on the unity of the socialist state we will destroy."

The following year, Stalin ended the purges by purging the torturers and secret policemen who had made it happen. The "association in which the free development of each is the condition for the free development of all" that had been predicted by Marx and Engels in the *Communist Manifesto* had failed to emerge. Instead, a new frightened, dull generation of bureaucrats had risen from the overthrow of the bourgeoisie, and would—in the generations to come—settle down to the indolence and mild corruption that eventually undermined Russian communism.

The *Manifesto* Beyond Soviet Russia

Those who had been inspired by the *Manifesto* and Marx's other writings were thrilled by the events in Russia, turning a blind eye to the violence and the official brutality. Some of the greatest thinkers of the world made their way to Moscow, and many pronounced themselves excited as well by Soviet achievements in literacy and women's liberation. They waited to see how the dream of international revolution set out by Marx and Engels would spread. It did not. There were moments when the hearts of the faithful swelled in hope, but somehow it never quite happened.

The closest anywhere else in Europe came to Marxist revolt was in Germany in the aftermath of defeat in World War I, when a general strike paralyzed the country in January 1919. "Act! Act courageously, decisively and consistently," wrote the revolutionary Leninist Rosa Luxemburg, while at the same time denouncing the idea of undisciplined and spontaneous uprisings. "Disarm the counter-revolution, arm the masses, occupy all positions of power. Act quickly!"

International communism's most prominent martyr, Rosa Luxemburg did not survive the German revolution that she reluctantly launched in 1919. The uprising was uncompromisingly suppressed.

But it was not enough. The private armies under the control of the minister of defense recaptured the police headquarters in Berlin and brutally suppressed any other gatherings that looked likely to result in uprising. In that month's democratic elections—the first ever in Germany—the Independent Socialist Party won just 7 percent of the vote.

Also in 1919, the Russian Communist Party launched the International, known as the Comintern, to link and coordinate the emerging communist parties around Europe. The abortive revolutions later on in Hungary and Munich were regarded as a failure and became fodder for the ongoing struggle between Stalin and Trotsky. Until the outbreak of World War II, Comintern policy veered between the two extremes. Sometimes it reflected Trotsky's policy of a

The Bonus March of World War I veterans who besieged Washington in 1932 at the height of the Great Depression. Even the near collapse of the American banking system did not bring about Marx's predicted revolution.

united front with other socialist parties—and the way that German communists bracketed their social democrat rivals with the Nazis arguably assisted Hitler to power. At other times it reflected Stalin's policy to make the Comintern virtually a front organization for narrow Soviet diplomacy. Ordinary Communist Party members across the world were expected to accommodate each twist, up to and including the notorious pact between Hitler and Stalin in 1939, which carved up Poland between them.

In France, Léon Blum's Popular Front was included in the government, and communists played a role in the republican government in Spain—holding out during the siege of Madrid against the Fascist forces of General Francisco Franco. But both played minor roles while non-revolutionary socialist parties usually took center stage.

In Britain, the tiny Communist Party managed to arrange the election of one of its members to Parliament. The ideas behind the *Communist Manifesto*—state ownership of land and industry, free education, progressive tax—were mobilized most successfully by socialist parties that had rejected Marx's call to revolution. For the most part they believed in social reform and gradual improvement through the existing democratic system.

The 1926 General Strike in Britain provided an opportunity, although Marxist revolutionaries were soon disappointed about press reports of strikers playing soccer with police. The Great Depression that followed provided some of the conditions for possible revolution on both sides

of the Atlantic. Both the Jarrow March in Britain and the 1932 Bonus March in the United States, which brought hungry former soldiers to camp in Washington, included communists who subscribed to every word of the *Manifesto*. But they were outnumbered by ordinary socialists, social reformers, and humanitarians. And both events were ignored by the presiding governments.

Marxist revolutionaries provided the world with some of the heroes of the Left in those years, such as the Americans Joe Hill ("Takes more than bullets to kill a man;/ I never died, said he") and John Reed, author of *Ten Days That Shook the World*. Or La Pasionaria (Dolores Ibarruri), the heroine of the Spanish Civil War, which brought tens of thousands of young men from all over the world to fight on the side of the republicans in the 1930s.

One of these was the English writer and socialist George Orwell, whose experience of the confusion and bitter violence of communist command in Spain—outlined in his book *Homage to Catalonia*—planted the seeds of doubt in his mind. Orwell provided the most devastating critique of totalitarian Marxism in practice in his novels *Animal Farm* and *1984*, with its terrifying portrayal of life under Big Brother. Orwell's novels reveal what happens when a person claims for himself the absolute power to rule on behalf of someone else. As a commentary on the *Communist Manifesto*, which envisages rule on behalf of the proletariat —and is hazy about how this might be achieved—Orwell's writings were, and remain, devastating.

George Orwell's books *Animal Farm* and *Homage to Catalonia*, which in different genres provided a devastating critique of what communism and totalitarianism actually meant in practice.

Marx's portrait presides over a meeting of Chinese communists during Mao's mythic Long March, which took his followers on an exhausting 6,000-mile trek out of the clutches of their nationalist rivals.

The *Manifesto* in China

Marx and Lenin never met, and would probably have agreed on little if they had. But one area of agreement would have been the subject that so exercised the minds of Stalin and his rivals in Russia. Neither man believed that the peasantry could be the engine of revolution: for both of them the key drivers were the industrial proletariat. Peasants were irrelevant at best; at worst they were an obstacle to revolutionary progress. But in China, Mao Zedong proved them wrong.

There was no official communist party in China until 1921—when it boasted 57 members. In the early years of Chinese communism, only one of the party's leaders could understand German. The others had to read the *Communist Manifesto* and Marx's other writings in translation—or learn about it in lectures. There was no translation of *Das Kapital* into Chinese until the 1930s and there is no evidence that Mao ever read it.

In fact Mao rarely quoted from Marx. "There are so many arguments in Marxism," he wrote. "We can summarize them all, in the final analysis, in one sentence: to rebel is justified." And yet he knew enough about Marx to realize that he was diverging from the *Manifesto* when he declared that, in China, the peasants were the revolutionary class. Like Lenin, Mao also urged extreme measures: "Revolution is not a dinner party," he wrote. "It is not like writing an essay, or doing embroidery. It cannot be so refined, so leisurely and gentle, so temperate, kind, courteous, restrained, and magnanimous.

Mao Zedong in 1944, fighting a war on two fronts—against Chiang Kai-shek and the nationalists, and against invading Japanese forces. The Japanese were gone the following year, and the nationalists were forced off the mainland five years later.

To right a wrong, we must exceed the 'proper' limits." Unlike his Soviet counterparts, Mao never allowed himself to stop pushing at those proper limits—hence his famous maxim that political power "grows out of the barrel of a gun."

Communism came to China in 1949, not by revolution, but by old-fashioned military victory. Mao and his party had driven out the Japanese, who had invaded in 1937, and had, after many years of civil war, dispatched the rival nationalists under Chiang Kai-shek to Taiwan.

Like Stalin, Mao started by moving against the landed gentry and richer peasants with a series of show trials, killing around two million of them and forcing the rest to endure what became known as "re-education," or the even more terrible "reform" camps. Private property was outlawed, and private companies—those that had survived two decades of war—were nationalized. Many of Mao's early efforts resulted in the same kind of disaster as Stalin's. His so-called "Great Leap Forward" campaign, depending for its success on rigid and unimaginative local party tyrants, ended in a disastrous famine that starved some 20 million people to death.

There was also tension with his communist comrades in Russia. Mao and Nikita Khrushchev, Stalin's successor, heartily disliked each other. When Khrushchev finally condemned Stalinism in 1956, Mao was taken completely by surprise. The following year he predicted that the "east wind prevails over the west wind"—meaning that his style of communism would eventually win over the Russian style.

The Russians rejected the idea, complaining that the words were "wholly without Marxist-Leninist content."

Mao sank into the background as his regime settled down in the 1960s, but surged back in 1966 with his extraordinary Cultural Revolution—his own response to the kind of lazy corruption to which Soviet communism had also descended. This was a further twist to the original vision of Marx and Engels, and involved chanting Red Guards, each with their "Little Red Book" of Mao's remarks; the browbeating of teachers by their pupils; communes taking control in the main cities; and as many as 17 million young people being sent from the cities to work in the countryside.

It was a period of fanaticism that may have resulted in the deaths of as many as 400,000 people, led by a "Gang of Four" that included Mao's actress wife Jiang Qing. When she was finally arrested in 1976 (less than a month after Mao's death) more than one million people celebrated on the streets of Shanghai alone. But China was inherited by the wily Deng Xiaoping, who managed to combine totalitarian brutality and pragmatism in almost equal measure.

Under Deng, the regime hung on to the trappings of totalitarian rule, including fearsome street committees that were its eyes and ears, and more than 100 million loudspeakers in the homes of peasants, broadcasting party music and information. And on June 4, 1989—just as communism was starting to unravel in Europe—he made his position clear when some 2,600 demonstrators were massacred by the army in Beijing's Tiananmen Square.

China's accelerating economy may, in the twenty-first century, have opened up to trade, and a tiny percentage of the population may enjoy privileges unprecedented anywhere else in the world, but—though it resembles nothing in the *Communist Manifesto*—China is still nominally a communist state. For the time being.

Mao's successor Deng Xiaoping. Under Deng, China remained communist and totalitarian, but opened up to trade in a way that would have horrified Marx, Lenin, or Mao. The paradox remains today.

The Cold War and the Events of 1989

As Soviet troops picked their way through the suburbs of the Hungarian capital, the three wartime leaders, Churchill, Roosevelt, and Stalin, were putting the finishing touches on their agreement in Yalta in February 1945 that would carve up Europe between them and pave the way for the communist domination of Eastern Europe after the war. It was the most important in a series of summit meetings that began in Casablanca (to which Stalin was not invited) and ended in Potsdam, finishing with an agreement that the United Nations should be set up and that occupied countries should be free and democratic. Churchill was furious that Roosevelt and Stalin managed such cordial relations at his expense, and it soon became clear that Stalin's definition of "free" included subordination to Moscow.

In this way, the great division of Europe that led to the Cold War came about, with Russian-backed communist parties taking power—often in the most brutal way—in Warsaw, Prague, Budapest, Bucharest, Tirana, and the other capitals of the Eastern Bloc. Non-communist parties were dissolved, and potential rival leaders were

disposed of (Czechoslovakia's Jan Masaryk was almost certainly thrown out the window of his office in 1948). Dismal puppet Stalinists were given the keys of office. Twice, Soviet tanks intervened to enforce their rule—in Hungary in 1956 and Czechoslovakia in 1968—after popular uprisings or political thawings threatened to overthrow the local *nomenklatura* or their ideas.

The revolution envisaged in the *Communist Manifesto* was supposed to be inevitable and permanent. Marx and Engels had not foreseen such eventualities—and certainly not the extraordinary growth of the clearly anticommunist proletarian trade union Solidarity in Poland in the 1980s.

In Yugoslavia, where Marshal Tito's Marxist guerrillas effectively took control of the country without the aid of Russian troops, yet another version of Marxism was to emerge. Soon Tito and Stalin were denouncing each other, and Tito's ministers were asked to read Marx and carve out a different approach to the Moscow line. The result was "decentralization" (factories "belonging to the workers"), "debureaucratization," and "worker's self-management." The Yugoslavs also rolled back the Stalinist principle of collective farms. It was a more humane and more successful style of communism, which, however, hid the vitriolic rival nationalisms that simmered below the surface of Yugoslavia.

When Stalin challenged the West by closing West Berlin to the outside world in 1948, it was supplied with as much as 8,000 tons of necessities every day by air in order to survive. It was 14 years before the Cold War got its ultimate symbol in the Berlin Wall, which divided the city in half. The Iron Curtain—Churchill's term—created a deepening suspicion of communism in the West, with the two sides staring at each other across the frontier that separated East and West.

By then it was clear that—even if it had never been true before—the famous opening lines of the *Communist Manifesto*, claiming that "a specter is haunting Europe" in the shape of communism, had finally become a reality. The trouble was that wherever communism had become a genuine specter, the authorities (as during the Paris Commune) reacted with irrational brutality. And if they failed to prevent communists from seizing power, as they did in Portugal after the demise of the country's military dictatorship, the angry crowds—the weapon that the *Manifesto* imagined would be supporting communist revolution—made sure they progressed no further.

Nowhere was this more true than in America. In Latin America, communists—and radicals of all kinds—were brutally murdered by military regimes. In the United States, a witch hunt against an almost nonexistent communist threat was whipped into hysteria by the sinister Senator Joe McCarthy. The Cold War was brought closer to home for the United States not so much by the regular Soviet spy scares as by the emergence of a Marxist guerrilla leader in Cuba called Fidel Castro—and by a standoff between the two neighbors that nearly brought the world to nuclear annihilation, thanks to the 1962 Cuban Missile Crisis.

Top: **Cuba's revolutionary leader Fidel Castro in 1957, when he was still fighting in the jungle.**

Above: **Ho Chi Minh saddles a mule in 1945, preparing for action against the French colonial rulers of Vietnam.**

Cold War theorists developed a worldview that saw communism as an indivisible bloc plotting slow revolution everywhere. This was the so-called Domino Theory, the idea that allowing one country to fall into communist hands would cause a cascade across the world, and it was used to justify almost any expenditure, or to support any dictator who seemed strong enough to resist them. "He may be a son of a bitch," President Roosevelt is supposed to have said of the Nicaraguan dictator Anastasio Somoza, "but he's our son of a bitch."

Although, in reality, the two main players in the communist bloc—Russia and China—deeply distrusted each other, the urgency of the Domino Theory led first United Nations troops into action in the Korean War, and then US and Australian troops against communist insurgents in North Vietnam. The tragedy of the Vietnam War led to horrific slaughter on both sides, including the terrible misery inflicted on civilians by bombing Vietnam and Cambodia. It was a brutalizing process that must have contributed to the rise of one of the most murderous communist regimes of them all: that of Pol Pot, whose Khmer Rouge fanatics killed at least two million as they forcibly emptied the cities to "purify" the population by transforming them back into peasants. It represented a complete reversal of Marx and Engels's support for the industrial proletariat.

In practice, the Domino Theory was wrong, but that became clear only with hindsight. In the mid-1970s, when Vietnam, Cambodia, and Laos rapidly succumbed to communist regimes, Marxism seemed unstoppable.

The policy of the former imperialist powers of Europe, to hand over their empires to moderate leaders, seemed to break down under the pressure of the Cold War, leading either to vicious Western-supported warlords taking control or vicious Eastern-supported Marxists.

It may not have been necessary. Even Ho Chi Minh—the fanatical inspiration behind revolution in Vietnam—worked hard for an American alliance in his early days. Yet the emergence of Marxist guerrilla movements across Africa and Latin America—not to mention the brutal Marxist-Leninist generals in control of Burma (now Myanmar)—was not enough by the 1980s to cover up the extent of communism's failure in the places where it had ruled longest. In Russia and its Eastern European satellites, life was increasingly dour as the mixed economies spiraled into decline and inefficiency—suffocated by the black market, and unreformable because the systems allowed no dissent. Intricate systems of state surveillance and betrayal were built into every detail of the lives of individuals: there were 125 miles of files in the Stasi secret-police headquarters in East Berlin alone.

The emergence of Mikhail Gorbachev as Soviet general secretary in 1984 and the rapid reform over which he presided—followed by the collapse of the Berlin Wall in 1989, and of most of the nominally Marxist regimes in Eastern Europe—marked the end of the dreams set out 140 years earlier by Marx and Engels. It is hard to imagine what they would have made of the popular uprisings that cleared out the *nomenklatura*, and of the dancing on the ruins of the Wall.

Top: the terrible consequences of totalitarian rule: a pile of skulls in a deserted Cambodian school, a legacy of the rule of Pol Pot.

Above: Mikhail Gorbachev and Ronald Reagan meeting at the Geneva Summit in 1985, just four years before the collapse of the Berlin Wall.

The collapse of communism as a serious alternative model for the world at the end of the 1980s was not exactly sudden, but equally it would not have been predicted even 15 years before. The loss of the Vietnam War and the fall of Saigon represented a major defeat for the United States as the leader of the anticommunist states in the West—and so was the Soviet invasion of Afghanistan in the winter of 1979—and for a while it looked as though the Domino Theory was all too correct.

This was even the case in Europe, where a new brand of Marxism—known as "Eurocommunism" and distancing itself from the excesses of Stalinist rule—began to develop, thanks to the efforts of the Spanish Civil War veteran Santiago Carrillo, whose book *Eurocommunism and the State* was published, with enormous influence, in 1976. Carrillo and his followers defended human rights, accepted the continued existence of the private sector, and aroused the fury of purist Marxists by pointing out how inequalities continued even in the Soviet Union. Most of all—flying in the face of the thrilling principle of revolution in the *Communist Manifesto*—they agreed to accept the verdict of voters if they were democratically ejected from power.

For a while it seemed as though the specter that Marx and Engels had described as "stalking Europe" was still haunting it. But Europe's communist parties began to divide, and their share of the vote—even from the high point of 34 percent in Italy—began to slip. Even the victorious communists of Vietnam soon discovered, behind the façade

Rebel soldiers in Ethiopia in 1991 take on the forces of the Marxist government under Mengistu Haile Mariam.

erected by their government, that production was crumbling, rice harvests were falling, and people were starving. They soon began to notice that tens of thousands of their own people were risking their lives in tiny boats across the China Sea just to escape living under a Marxist regime.

It was in the guerrilla movements of Southeast Asia, Africa, and Latin America that the original principles of the *Manifesto* remained stubbornly alive. Often these armed insurrections were supported by Cuban or Russian military aid or intervention, which quickly led to bitter civil wars—as in Yemen and Ethiopia—which in turn led to famine and serious debt and the economic decline of whole continents. Sometimes they were fanned into life in the first place by the fearful repression of fervently anticommunist military rulers.

Marx's specter worked both ways. It was fear of Marx and Engels and their influence that was just as much a cause of the counter-insurgents, funded by Cold War warriors in the West, as it was a cause of the Marxist revolutionaries. These counter-insurgents supported brutal military regimes in Chile, Argentina, Brazil, and Uruguay, as well as Africa—with the widespread and secret use of torture and death squads—and the overthrow of Latin America's only democratically elected Marxist president, Chile's Salvador Allende.

Quietly, and almost without the world noticing, the actual fighting of the Cold War was shifted onto the poorest populations of the world, because they represented the hopes and fears of both sides. These miserable wars

The leader of Peru's Maoist guerilla movement, the Shining Path, is presented to the press after his capture in 1992. The appalling violence of the guerillas was matched only by that of the government forces ranged against them.

and repressions were as much a result of the publication of the *Communist Manifesto* a century and a quarter before as any of the rest.

It will be remembered as a brutal period of history. In Nicaragua, the Marxist-Leninist Sandinistas won a temporary victory, until pushed back by U.S.-financed and armed rebels. In Peru, the ferocious Maoist Shining Path guerrillas inspired a vitriolic campaign by government forces that outdid even them in brutality. These were patterns repeated on every continent, but somehow especially in Africa—where South Africa, under its policy of apartheid, had suppressed the Communist Party since 1950, wrongly dismissing their nationalist opponents in the ANC as a communist front organization.

Right across Africa, the Cold War wafted into power communist despots and Western-backed military dictators, each side despoiling a continent that had embraced independence with such hope. But the greatest progress made there by Marxists was in territory controlled by the European power that had clung to its empire longest—the Portuguese. The result was Marxist governments and long-running civil wars that devastated former Portuguese colonies such as Mozambique, Angola, and Guinea-Bissau.

Once Mikhail Gorbachev had succeeded in his dramatic reforms, and the liberation of Eastern Europe had become a reality, with China swallowing certain aspects of capitalism, only a few strongholds such as Cuba held out against the tide—and without Soviet support, their

resources did not stretch to financing global revolution. With the end of the Cold War, the engine behind so many of the guerrilla wars disappeared, and it was possible to broker peace deals—and to reassure South Africans sufficiently to dismantle their apartheid system and let their population finally elect the ANC.

The end of wide-scale Marxism did not just undermine the remaining communist totalitarian regimes; it also made it possible for the world to lose patience with non-communist totalitarianism. It is a strange irony that where the communist revolution set out by Marx and Engels failed to liberate the proletariat, the failure of the revolution was able to provide a measure of liberation in some of the most despairing corners of the world.

The world's remaining notorious Marxists: Zimbabwe's president Robert Mugabe at an election rally in 2000 (above), and the father-and-son rulers of North Korea (top), Kim-Il Sung and Kim Jong Il, in 1995.

So it was that, by the 1990s, the only regimes left that professed to rule by the principles laid out in the *Manifesto* were a bizarre and unattractive bunch, including Zimbabwe under Robert Mugabe's corrupt one-party state, as well as Vietnam and Cambodia, and the closed world of Burma (Myanmar). The most odious of all was the continuing regime in North Korea, which even China viewed with suspicion, and which cut itself off from the world and appeared to be facing increasing starvation under Kim-Il Sung's son Kim Jong Il, who took over after the death of his father in 1994 as if he were an old-fashioned monarch.

It was further evidence, if any was needed, of the peculiar way in which the principles of the *Manifesto* led not to international revolution but to fervent nationalism. But the

A mud-spattered portrait of Serbia's Slobodan Milosevic in Belgrade, before his ejection from power. For some reason, Marxism has tended in practice to transmute into fervent nationalism.

final proof was much nearer home, in the figure of Slobodan Milosevic, whose succession to power in Marxist Yugoslavia quickly transmuted itself into a bitter Serbian nationalism, and whose rule was finally ended after a brutal civil war and military intervention in Kosovo by NATO forces.

The Survival of Marxism

Looking back at the century and a half of Marxism, it is clear that the principles that Marx and Engels set down have become discredited. The vision of East Germans dancing on the ruins of the Berlin Wall, which had trapped them inside a puritanical Marxist-Leninist dictatorship, was enough to dispel any continuing illusions among the vast majority of the world. So it is easy now to forget that, for much of the middle third of the twentieth century, nearly four out of ten people in the world were ruled by governments that claimed to be Marxist.

Marx would probably have recognized none of them as the kind of society he was hinting at—the *Manifesto* was vague about what they were actually striving toward after the revolution. In fact, Marx was just the kind of intellectual who would have been an early victim of one of Stalin's purges.

What is ironic about this whole episode in world history is that the most successful followers of the principles of the *Manifesto*—Lenin, Stalin, and Mao—were single-minded students of the politics of power, and used Marx's ideas as a rationale for taking it and keeping it. As we have seen, their rule afterward was as much about exploiting nationalism as it was about Marxist ideology. The contemporary Marxist historian Eric Hobsbawm argues that, actually, Marxism was never really put to the test. But the collapse of communism around the world—and the terrible damage wrought by the ideology on any nations rash enough to try it—reveals serious flaws and contradictions at the heart of the *Communist Manifesto*.

Despite this, the specter of communism is still alive. And it is kept alive partly by those who have a vested interest in doing so. Conservatives are often prepared to help extremists on the other side to power, for fear of the communists. For those on the political Right who want to take power themselves—or just sell arms to those who want to take power; or pass restrictive legislation—it makes sense to talk up the Marxist threat.

Marxism has also remained alive among academics as a critique of industrial alienation. Marx and Engels are alive in academic debate in a way in which they are no longer alive in politics: for those who valued action above thought, this would not have pleased them.

The Survival of the *Manifesto*
The *Communist Manifesto* is one of the most-published books in the world. It is possible that it has appeared in print more than almost any other book except for the Bible and the Koran. In fact there were 544 editions in 35 languages even before the Russian Revolution in 1917. As the most popular outline of Marxism, it still sells widely all over the world.

Despite the collapse of communism, it is possible to see the legacy of Marx and Engels everywhere. There may be few Marxist governments in power, but it is now impossible to look at any corner of modern history, sociology, philosophy, or the arts without seeing the fingerprints of the authors of the *Manifesto*.

Because, if you set aside the predictions that failed to materialize, and the vague calls to violent revolution that unhappily did, there is an enduring critique at the heart of the *Manifesto* that lives on. It was Marx, after all, who first saw human history as the story of the grip over humanity of the power of money.

We might take with a grain of salt the *Manifesto*'s claim that the working class is the instrument that will liberate humanity from its power, but we still have to take seriously the other claim: that the power of capital has alienated human beings from each other and from themselves. That is the continuing importance of the *Manifesto*: what the philosopher Peter Singer calls "a vision of human beings in a state of alienation."

Actually the word "alienation" appears only once, but that is what is meant. The bourgeoisie, according to the *Manifesto*, "has resolved personal worth into exchange value, and in place of the numberless indefeasible chartered freedoms, has set up that single, unconscionable freedom—Free Trade. In one word, for exploitation, veiled by religious and political illusions, it has substituted naked, shameless, direct, brutal exploitation."

One might not agree with the critique, but it is as fresh and relevant as ever—and as disturbing. Modern society likes to emphasize how capitalists and the workforce have interests in common—both sides need investment to get jobs, after all. They prefer to avoid Marx's dictum that the two sides are fundamentally opposed, and that the workforce is actually the instrument that will overthrow the whole system.

It is true, also, that if you look at developed nations, with their batteries of employment laws, the *Manifesto*'s claim that capital pays workers just enough to keep them alive seems ridiculous. Even a century ago Henry Ford understood that he had to pay his workforce enough for them to afford the products they were creating. But a glimpse at some of the results of globalization—the sweatshops of Nicaragua or Bangladesh—makes the claim seem only too relevant. As many as 150 years after Marx and Engels, you can still find people at work six days a week, ten hours a day, making clothes for global companies, sewing pairs of jeans at a unit cost of about 20 cents a pair (including wages) that retail in the United States for up to $30.

Still relevant also are the *Manifesto*'s ideas about history. At Marx's funeral—with just 11 mourners in an obscure corner of Highgate Cemetery in London—Engels described his achievement as the discovery of a scientific law of human history that could be compared to Darwin's breakthrough in biology. This was the idea that history had somehow gone its own sweet way all these centuries, while ignoring the engine that drove it along. "History was for the first time placed on its real basis," wrote Engels later, "the palpable but previously overlooked fact that men must first of all eat, drink, have shelter and clothing, therefore must *work*, before they can fight for domination, pursue politics, religion, philosophy, etc.—this palpable fact at last came into its historical rights."

Before Marx, history was about heroes, kings, princesses, and magnates. After Marx, the people who made it possible for them to live were given their rightful place. History was made three-dimensional for the first time.

But then, the *Manifesto* goes too far, even in its opening statement: "The history of all hitherto existing society is the history of class struggles." There is no doubt that the insight provided historians with a powerful tool for looking at the tectonic shifts of human progress, and the rise and fall of civilizations. But no interpretation as simple as that can possibly do justice to the full complexity of humanity. Religion and morality remain critical engines of human development. Feudalism had as much to do with military needs as material ones.

Sometimes, in other words, our behavior cannot be entirely understood in terms of class struggle—any more than it could be completely understood by a Darwinian or a Freudian. Sometimes human beings rise above any ideology that tries to squeeze them—and if we listen hard enough, the voices of history will confirm this experience, once we take off our basic Marxist blinkers.

In his later years Marx claimed that this ideological approach to history was a misinterpretation of what he actually said. He just wanted to emphasize the economic motivations of history, not claim that somehow it was the only determining factor. "All I know," an endlessly irritable Marx told Engels, "is that I am not a Marxist."

That may be so, but reading the *Manifesto* today makes it all too clear that his predictions about history (based on little more than a hunch)—that the rise of the bourgeoisie was bound to be followed by the dictatorship of the proletariat—seems to have been disproved by actual events many times over.

Marx talked about communism as "the riddle of history solved." Actually he did not solve the riddle of history. Nobody has. And the prevailing view is that it has no meaning in it at all—but he did set the riddle more clearly, and for that he is rightly honored.

That would not have been enough for him, because for Marx, action was more important than philosophy—the number of times the words "action" or "reaction" occurs in the *Manifesto* is proof enough of this. One of the theses of the philosopher Ludwig Feuerbach, who influenced Marx enormously as he developed his ideas, is carved on his tomb: "The philosophers have only interpreted the world in various ways; the point is, to change it." Marx did change the world, but not in the way he expected or intended. There was no culmination of history, but his interpretations and the questions that arise out of them still remain.

New Influences

Some of the ideas in the *Manifesto* have, in the late twentieth and early twenty-first century, taken on a new political life.

Marx was no environmentalist. Everything in the *Manifesto* assumes that the Earth is infinite and productivity endless. He is not interested in limits to the planet, just in limits to the way the bourgeois economy distributes it. Yet the idea that money alienates human beings is a powerful aspect of the modern Green critique around the world, which argues that there are more important things. The concept of economic growth—measuring success according to the money value going through a national economy—was not invented in Marx's lifetime, but you can see echoes of his writings in the modern criticism of it. Life is more than money, say modern antiglobalization campaigners: there are many aspects of life that money just cannot encapsulate.

In the same way, the rise of fair trade and ethical investment, the "ethical" trademarks in supermarkets all over the Western world, are in some ways the antithesis of Marxism—the *Manifesto* reserves special condemnation for what Marx called the "Utopian Socialism" of Robert Owen and others. He would say such things were simply keeping the existing order in place, to save society from revolution rather than hastening it along. But they are also a symptom of the Marx and Engels analysis—that human relations can, and must, go beyond money.

We are in a state of alienation because we are controlled by a money system that seems outside anyone's power, said the *Manifesto*. We forget that it is a product of humankind. But that same idea emerges in some of the programs for government even of conservative parties around the world, defending family and community against the ravages of the market.

If Marx was no environmentalist, he equally was no idealist—like those hated "Utopian Socialists" who had schemes for the amelioration of working conditions. But his ideas emerge one and a half centuries later in the ideal of disconnecting work from money, so that people can work not because they dare not stop and starve, but because they love it—as Marx put it, so that work might "not only be a means of life, but life's prime want." That was why he was able to predict so idealistically in the *Manifesto* that the state would cease to exist under communism, to be replaced by what he calls "an association, in which the free development of each is the condition for the free development of all." It was idealistic and, as history would prove, miserably wrong.

Yet when modern campaigners object to the way that one model of individual ownership—from the enclosure of commons to intellectual property in genes—is driving out some of the older ways of understanding property, they are reflecting a little of that idealism from the *Manifesto*. And when they sigh and remember the way that medieval societies were more able to own property in common (whether it was the field their cattle grazed, the common oven, or the common bull), they are in a way reflecting Marx's critique.

When Marx described capital as "dripping from head to foot from every pore, with blood and dirt," he was talking of child labor, of cottage industries deliberately ruined, of the destruction of the commons, and of out-of-work former small-farm owners forced into urban factories to survive. When he talked about the inevitable mergers of corporate capitalism, the tendency of modern economies to undermine competition, allowing companies to combine into fewer and fewer increasingly monopolistic enterprises, that prediction is only too obviously true 150 years later.

And yet, Marx was wrong too often. His prediction that capitalism would collapse under its own internal contradictions has failed to take place—though it has tottered occasionally. He was wrong too in saying that the system always drives wages lower and that it requires armies of unemployed paupers to succeed. But the basic thrust of his critique of industrial economics is still in use today: when antiglobalization campaigners use arguments about the basic contradictions in global corporate power, they are reflecting the path first carved out by the *Communist Manifesto*. And when modern politicians—whether they are liberal or green, socialist or conservative—complain that capitalism is wasteful, destructive of human relationships, and out of control, they are echoing the criticisms of Marx and Engels. It's just that, after a century of watching Marxist governments find a better system, the chances are they will not follow the *Manifesto*'s preferred route toward an alternative.

Antiglobalization protesters in Paris in 2003. Antiglobalization campaigns reflect some of Marx and Engels's critique of the power of money over life—though not, these days, their preferred solution.

Old-fashioned communists at a rally in Brussels in 2001, using the familiar image of the Cuban Marxist Che Guevara.

The central problem is that, if we have to coerce people into acting for the collective good, rather than just the individual good, then the flaws in the *Manifesto* become clear. Coercion meant that Marxism in practice replaced one ruling class with another; it meant that the alienation that Marx wanted to destroy remained as powerful as ever.

None of this means that, as some critics have said about the *Manifesto*, we must simply accept a society that embraces a brutal and selfish form of individualism—for Marx and Engels's critique of that kind of alienation remains true. It is just that 150 years later we are all very suspicious of their vague revolutionary solution, with its fatal hint of violence.

THE COMMUNIST MANIFESTO
FURTHER READING AND WEB SITES

Further Reading

Berlin, Isaiah, *Karl Marx: His Life and Environment*, Oxford and New York: Oxford University Press, 1996.

Hunley, J. D., *The Life and Achievements of Friedrich Engels*, New Haven: Yale University Press, 1991.

McLellan, David, *The Young Hegelians and Karl Marx*, Aldershot: Ashgate Publishing, 1993.

Pipes, Richard, *Communism: A History*, New York: Modern Library, 2001.

Scribner, Charity, *Requiem for Communism*, Cambridge, M.A.: MIT Press, 2003.

Segal, Boris M., *Karl Marx: The Apostle of Hate and the Marxist Legacy*, Bloomington: 1st Books Library, 2003.

Service, Robert, *Russia: Experiment with a People*, Cambridge, M.A.: Harvard University Press, 2003.

Tucker, Robert C. (ed.), *The Marx–Engels Reader*, New York: W. W. Norton & Company, 1978.

Wheen, Francis, *Karl Marx: A Life,* New York: W. W. Norton & Company, 2000.

Wolff, Jonathan, *Why Read Marx Today?*, Oxford and New York: Oxford University Press, 2003.

Web Sites

Australia National University Marxism page
www.anu.edu.au/polsci/marx/marx.html

In Defence of Marxism
www.marxist.com

Karl Marx Literature Forum
www.topicsites.com/communist

Marx/Engels Internet Archive
www.ex.ac.uk/Projects/meia

Marxism Mailing List
www.marxmail.org

Marxists Internet Archive
www.marxists.org

THE COMMUNIST MANIFESTO
ACKNOWLEDGMENTS

David Boyle wishes to acknowledge all the help he has received
from Judith Hodge.

The author

David Boyle is a writer about politics, history, and ideas. He is the
author of *The Sum of Our Discontent* and a range of other titles. He is
married and lives in London.

The series editor

Neil Turnbull is currently senior lecturer in Social Theory
at Nottingham Trent University. He has published a book
and a variety of academic articles on the history and contemporary
cultural significance of philosophy, technology, and social theory.

Picture credits

The author and publisher are grateful to the following for permission
to reproduce illustrations:

Cameron Collection: pp.9T, 12/13, 13, 14, 90.

Corbis: pp.8, 11B Archivo Iconografico, 12 Gianni Diagli Orti, 16
Robert Holmes, 17 Archivo Iconografico, 21 E. O. Hoppe, 87, 89L
Gianni Diagli Orti, 92 Robert Estall, 109R, 109T Michael Freeman,
111 J. A. Giodano, 112 Balaguer Alejandro/Sygma, 113 Sygma, 113B
Silva Joao, 114 Kontos Yannis/Sygma, 117 Michael S. Yamashita,
122 Antoine Serra/In Visu, 123 Antoine Serra.

Corbis Bettmann Archive: pp.100, 103, 104, 105, 106L, 108T.

Corbis/Hulton-Deutsch Collection: pp.15T, 15B, 78, 79, 86, 89R, 94,
96, 97, 106T, 108B.

Library of Congress Prints and Photographs Division: pp.22, 74, 77,
88, 93T, 95, 96T, 98.